perspectives
ON DESIGN

design philosophies expressed by minnesota's leading professionals

Published by

PANACHE
PANACHE PARTNERS

1424 Gables Court
Plano, TX 75075
469.246.6060
Fax: 469.246.6062
www.panache.com

Publishers: Brian G. Carabet and John A. Shand

Printed in China

Distributed by Independent Publishers Group
800.888.4741

PUBLISHER'S DATA

Perspectives on Design Minnesota

Library of Congress Control Number: 2009922812

ISBN 13: 978-1-933415-77-2
ISBN 10: 1-933415-77-0

First Printing 2009

10 9 8 7 6 5 4 3 2 1

Right: Keenan & Sveiven, page 245
Previous Page: Meyer, Scherer & Rockcastle, Ltd., page 181

perspectives
ON DESIGN

design philosophies expressed by minnesota's leading professionals

introduction

Spizzi Mosaics, page 241

Aqua Eden, page 263

Creating the spaces in which we live and achieving the beauty we desire can be a daunting quest—a quest that is as diverse as each of our unique personalities. For some, it may be a serene, infinity-edge saltwater pool in the backyard; for others it may be an opulent marble entryway with bronze insets imported from Italy. Aspiring chefs may find a kitchen boasting the finest in technology their true sanctuary.

Perspectives on Design Minnesota is a pictorial journey from conceptualizing your dream home, to putting together the finishing touches, to creating an outdoor oasis. Alongside the phenomenal photography, you will have a rare insight to how these tastemakers achieve such works of art and be inspired by their personal perspectives on design.

Within these pages, the state's finest artisans share their wisdom, experience and talent. It is the collaboration between these visionaries and the outstanding pride and craftsmanship of the products showcased that together achieve the remarkable. Learn from leaders in the industry about the aesthetics of a finely crafted sofa, how appropriate lighting can dramatically change the appearance of a room and what is necessary to create a state-of-the-art home theater.

Whether your dream is to have a new home or one that has been redesigned to suit your lifestyle, *Perspectives on Design Minnesota* will be both an enjoyable journey and a source of motivation.

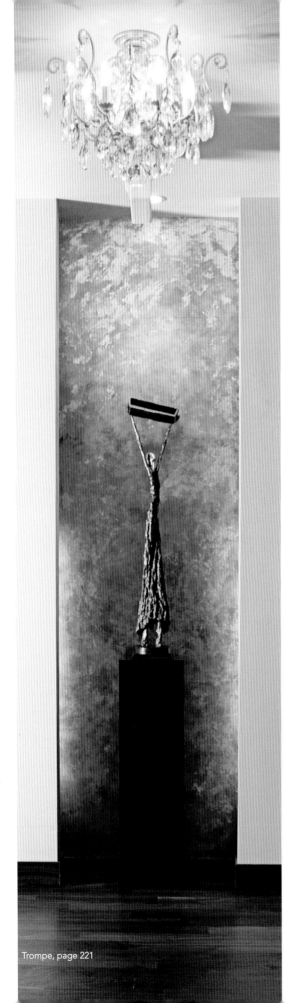

Trompe, page 221

contents

"Good design marries the interests of the upscale designer market with age-old tradition, while remaining committed to promoting respect for cultural expression and the environment. People can feel good about including aesthetic additions in their homes."

—Stephanie Odegard

Entertainment Designs, Inc., page 201

CF design ltd., page 15

MG McGrath Architectural Sheet Metal, page 157

Keenan & Sveiven, page 245

Meyer, Scherer & Rockcastle, Ltd., page 181

Cabinet Concepts and Interiors, page 193

Eskuche Creative Group, page 35

Cates Fine Homes, page 77

Earthscape Stone Masonry & Landscape Design, page 275

John Kraemer and Sons Inc., page 97

"Every aspect of a home should be a unique expression of its inhabitants."

—Charles R. Stinson

CF design ltd., page 15

Charles R. Stinson Architects, page 25

the concept

chapter one

Eskuche Creative Group, page 35

JDA Design Architects, page 45

SKD Architects, page 55

When an adventurous Minneapolis employer offered a career opportunity to Cheryl Fosdick more than 20 years ago, she took it—and hasn't looked back since. Now nurturing a strong, local residential market, Cheryl has pushed the region's interior taste to new levels as principal designer at CF design ltd. Strategic and thoughtful, her focus lies in mastering a balance between homeowner and site, pulling geographical factors and personal details to create the perfect space.

Minnesota offers an ideal environment to draw inspiration. The architecture embraces a certain drama found in the state's topography, making open home plans the most appealing and comprehensive. As a distinct intersection of aesthetics, Duluth offers visitors and residents its version of art history, visible in the built form. A transition from shipping port to travel destination over the last two decades has secured Duluth as a thriving possibility for architectural expansion, putting Cheryl's design know-how to work.

"I don't design around any particular style and I don't believe it serves as the essential generator of form. People often become stifled when they think in terms of specific styles. Cultural history and personal progressive nature work to determine likes and dislikes much more effectively than the traditions of a single approach."

—Cheryl Fosdick

CF DESIGN LTD.

ABOVE: A window is a frame and a point of departure from the wall. In an open bedroom, the head of the bed supports the canopy of the roof above; the windows then become curtains, defining enclosure. While only the bed is freestanding, the line between architecture and furniture is masterfully blurred.

FACING PAGE: The expression of the opening can define the window as a picture frame for a specific view or a diaphanous fabric of wood and glass, separating inside passages from outside terrain. Light pours through a home's glass, delineating night from day. When used properly, daylight becomes one of the most powerful tools of design. An abstract element becomes almost tangible, as designers have the ability to capture, direct and engineer the sun's rays.

PREVIOUS PAGES: What defines indoor and outdoor? These two environments do not begin and end with walls or partitions. Planes overhead define our limits of a perceived enclosure and the human scale within buildings. People gain comfort from knowing they are under something, surrounded by something—ceilings and walls are structurally believable. Playing off of this notion, I take advantage of ceiling planes that lay low to the ground to present an intimate slice of the surroundings. Essentially limitless on all sides, the space lets residents move easily and see from inside to outside beneath these enduring surfaces.

Photographs by Andrea Rugg

"Don't rush this process. In design, nothing done quickly is ever done well."

—Cheryl Fosdick

ABOVE: Minimalism has many interpretations. One view: it takes very little accommodation to comfortably and specifically inhabit a home. A chair at a table works as a vantage point and an opportunity to set aside time to appreciate the richness of people and place. Sitting in a chair quickly shifts perception. The texture and color of surfaces become more concentrated and pungent when at rest. I emphasize the importance of closeness and the contrasting distance of elements under controlled light. In this way, the mass of a fireplace can be interpreted as a mosaic of discreet stones, curiously balanced on the mantel.

FACING PAGE TOP: Creating outward views that include portions of the inhabited residence can camouflage the differences between inside and out. An indoor kitchen and the furniture of its island make up part of the greater outdoor dining space. Guests or homeowners could retire to the pillows of the quiet north court after a meal. I create a desire for the "place beyond" to organize the site's living spaces into a well-planned assembly.

FACING PAGE BOTTOM: Morning light is often the most poignant. Whether cast through an elegant stairwell or across a bedroom ceiling, morning light works best when the spaces and surfaces are set to receive it. An interior's palette develops through the understanding of daylight's effect: the shadows cast, texture of surfaces and variations of tone changes.
Photographs by Andrea Rugg

"Sympathy between program and site is essential. Simple feelings about fundamental things like daylight and the tactile or visual nature of specific materials must be carefully considered, all of which play off of the site and become part of the space."

—Cheryl Fosdick

ABOVE: Inside, simply, the outdoors inspire. Reflecting the dramatically fractured rocks and coulees of the Lake Superior North Shore, the fissured surface of the home's tall wall channels daylight from above, as the redwood stair falls away from the stone shelf of the floor like a river, toward a shaft of light between trees. As if on the water's edge, an embedded reed comprises the rails, along with recycled redwood from a local company. And for an innovative tub design wrapped by a second-floor stairwell clad in redwood, we achieved a warm wooden glow and borrowed from the clean beauty of the shower next door. Private and invisible to passersby, the space takes advantage of raw materials and transcends styles to create a carved-out look.

FACING PAGE: When a couple decided to embark on modern design within their home, they knew they were taking a leap of faith. Set on the westernmost point of the Great Lakes, our materials-driven interior selections reflect the nature of the surrounding outdoor elements. The offset third-bond travertine flooring gives a sense of shift and movement to the ground, as a gesture to the water, beach and sand. We took advantage of the space's ability to challenge the reality of human scale, juxtaposed with elements intimate as grass and wide as the blue-on-blue horizon lying just beyond the floor-to-ceiling windows.
Photographs by Andrea Rugg

"We are energized by the qualities of the place and remain thoroughly engaged by the landscape. Basalt outcroppings, dramatic inland seas, indistinct horizons of mirrored waters and skies, and leggy white pine forests provide fuel for our imaginations."

—Cheryl Fosdick

ABOVE: The master bedroom is a perfect example of our ability to minimize materials while maximizing the place. Pulling the eye over the distance of the long room, this space treats every attribute as if it were a piece of furniture. Built into the floor and wall, the bed sits with the shower and closet behind it. Not a single square inch is wasted, and supported by extraordinary craftsmanship, design takes center stage.

FACING PAGE TOP: For a rectangular condominium that measures just over 22 by 62 feet, every space is an equal part of a common ground. The whole really is greater than the sum of its parts, as each element—the island, stairways, cabinetry—are related in their furniture-like quality. Under foot and in hand, the same rich redwood that appears on the entry stair and handrail emerges as the wine cask envelops the private second-floor stairway and connects the two levels.

FACING PAGE BOTTOM LEFT: Thoughtfully knitted together, the condominium reveals the intention of each element. Simple things bring the space together: the repetitive vertical grain of the veneered cabinets depends on the horizontal wall pattern going up the stairwell. Contrast and proximity make this all work.

FACING PAGE BOTTOM RIGHT: A small bathroom carves opportunity out of the contrast of stone and glass, filling the space and creating a partition for the shower, both poetic and functional. We bounced high-wattage light to return without shadow to the vanity. Common stone accentuates the delicate and almost transitory nature of the sink and countertop—and of the reflected image in the mirror.

Photographs by Andrea Rugg

Are people born to pursue specific paths? Are we meant to do certain kinds of work? Charles Stinson's life seems to indicate so. His structures perfectly assimilate into rural and urban landscapes, revealing his gift to conceptualize and achieve the built form in any environment.

Charles has been highly visual since childhood, and his family knew that aesthetic design was in his future. More than 30 years of success has proven his family correct, as Charles has created residential and commercial buildings along with a master-planned community in an array of sites. His well-connected team of architects, interior designers and specialists make all this possible, working to influence, inspire and challenge one another.

Charles' architecture reveals where his interests lie—shapes, planes and nature. The three intersect in his designs, showing the strength of geometry and the careful combination of vertical and horizontal expansions. Organic elements quietly blend with his work, establishing a smooth indoor-outdoor relationship that has no beginning or end. Charles gives an effortless nod to his greatest inspirations: architectural icon Frank Lloyd Wright and modernist painter Charles Biederman. Influences from the two remain perpetually intertwined with every project.

"For years, I thought that architecture was about being inside the tree and carving holes out. But it's not. It's about living in the spaces between the branches."

—Charles R. Stinson

CHARLES R. STINSON ARCHITECTS

"The role of an interior designer is to fully understand the homeowner and the architecture while addressing the details—to pull it all together and make it work beautifully."

—Ruth Johnson

TOP: Working closely with interior designer Ruth Johnson of CRS Interiors, we created a home interior to complement the family as much as it does the geography of the site. Standing in the home's great room, visitors get a nautical sense, as if they are standing on a boat. Lake views fill the window and define the absence of a closed-off interior. The earth-toned décor reflects thoughtful choices; pendants add interest to the room without interfering with sightlines, keeping the room clear, clean and unobstructed.

BOTTOM: A large family who spends a good deal of time cooking required an open kitchen that fluidly connects with surrounding spaces. The wooden ceiling adds texture, warmth and blends in perfectly with the neutral tones—a background palette designed to showcase the homeowner's art collection.

PREVIOUS PAGES: When the couple disagreed about what style of house to build, it was suggested that they could have the best of both worlds. Combining the stimulation of simple, modern elements while maintaining warmth and comfort became a paramount balance, drawing from a limestone and wood palette. I visualized the space when the land sat empty, which is why the home's design fits perfectly into the waterside property.
Photographs by Peter Bastianelli-Kerze

"A home should reflect the residents' personalities, possess a human quality. Happy, vivid and full of life, my home is an unmistakable extension of me."

—Josh Stinson

ABOVE: Ruth knew that my son Josh would be the primary inspiration for the interior of his home. Brilliant and welcoming, the indoor-outdoor tones coordinate to give an overall uplifting effect. Bright greens and organic hues play against the exterior blues that make the house so eye-catching.

FACING PAGE: Once lodgings for nuns, the Minnesota farmhouse dates back 110 years. We had to gut the entire interior in order to restore it, but we were careful to preserve its historic elements, like the small, charming windows and a steep roofline. Jason of Stinson Builders, Inc. states: "Modern updates put the home at the forefront of design, embracing green principles. Solar panels, glass garage doors and a white metal roof make up elements that reveal keen planning and sustainable sophistication."

Photographs by Peter Bastianelli-Kerze

ABOVE: Located in Excelsior, Minnesota, a home intended as a retreat turned into the couple's year-round residence. The hillside lot allows the home perfect views of the lake and surrounding woodlands, while giving close-range sights of the trees, as well. Branches, leaves and verdant views mix with a sleek aesthetic to create treetop modernism. I floated the main level of the 3,300-square-foot home on top of a glass box—a simple composition of white horizontals and window ribbons bisected by gray chimneys and black window framing. The lower level houses guests' quarters, a media room, study area, studio and sauna. Designed to let natural light pour in, the home's light wells reveal keen orientation of the structure.

FACING PAGE: Nestled into the trees, the upper main floor features an open great room with window walls on the lakeside and transom windows opposite. A charcoal concrete-block fireplace accentuates the room's tree-top-high ceilings while offering a rich charcoal hue. The room maintains chic, clean lines and yet provides a calm, comfortable setting. Lush gray carpet provides a rich texture to the room, contrasting the sleek glass and smooth furniture throughout the space.
Photographs by Peter Bastianelli-Kerze

"Architecture should celebrate the human scale."

—Charles Stinson

"Climate and geography play a strong role in successful structures. Solar orientation, prevailing winds and seasonal climates are all critical in achieving the perfect composition."

—Charles Stinson

ABOVE: When building, we actually dug into the hillside. To enhance the home's treetop modernism, I designed a 12-foot-tall, charcoal-colored form, planted with small trees along the exterior of the great room. While the living room is elevated, the screened porch sits just below—a perfect spot to enjoy the sights and sounds of the lake.

FACING PAGE TOP: Jewel flecks of blue in the countertop give a slight, elegant shimmer to the surface. Asian influences appear throughout, including sustainable bamboo flooring and a Zen-like approach to spacing. Warmed with maple accents and a cozy breakfast nook, a state-of-the-art kitchen offers anything a home chef might need. A slim snack bar and island separates the kitchen from the dining area.

FACING PAGE BOTTOM: Continuing the tone of the home, the master bathroom provides a graceful space with modern aesthetics. Bathrooms are more than just a functional room; they serve as retreats and respites from life's stress.
Photographs by Peter Bastianelli-Kerze

The best homes endure for the same reasons beloved works of literature do—they place character above trends. They hook into people's dreams and passions, not the style of the moment.

Peter Eskuche homes are a perfect example of this. He's known as an architect who draws his inspiration directly from his clients to create dwellings that are as stunning for their beauty as they are for their personalities.

The process of creating a home with Peter is like a journey of discovery. Through questionnaires and meetings—some known to last as long as six hours—the architect works to understand a family's distinct style and character, exploring organizational habits, artistic views, what times of day they enjoy being together and more.

He translates this understanding into renderings, watercolors, and ultimately, a one-of-a-kind built environment designed to capture a family's character for generations to come.

"I spent my boyhood dreaming up tree houses, quirky spaces and impossible shelter designs. I think all those random dreams helped me build the creative resources I need to interpret my clients' dreams."

—Peter Eskuche

ESKUCHE CREATIVE GROUP

"A home's entrance is like a handshake. All the details should come together to make a one-of-a-kind impression."

—Peter Eskuche

LEFT: As we met with this family, it became clear from what they said, and even the way they spoke, that comfort and togetherness were important but that they appreciate privacy and security and are embraced by formality as well. So the home we designed for them presents itself as stately, yet is warm and inviting once entered. Raising the entrance and recessing it several feet was effective in providing the majestic and protective feel, while the layout is supported by themes of symmetry throughout.

PREVIOUS PAGES: The entrance is rustic and cozy, but it makes a strong impression. Natural stone, marble, Old World grilles over the windows and a substantial mahogany entry door give a sense of heft and history.
Photographs courtesy of Eskuche Creative Group

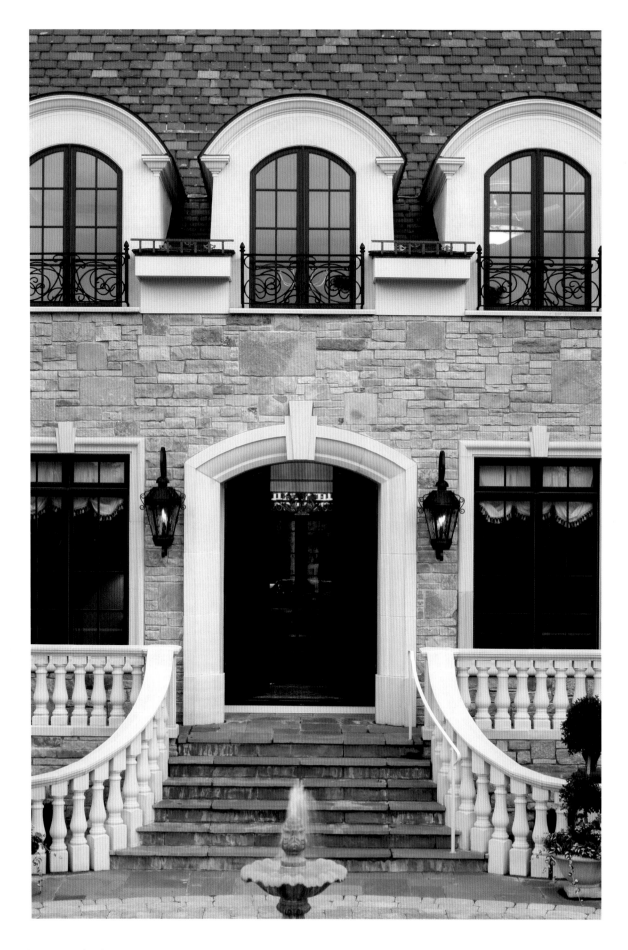

"I'm influenced less by a specific style or time period. I pull my inspiration, rather, from my clients' dreams…from who they are and how they live."

—Peter Eskuche

ABOVE: While the front of the home is elegant and proportioned, the back speaks to the family's love of comfort and togetherness. The intimacy is enhanced by warm, rich materials and abundant lighting. I understand the exterior porch has become a favorite space. There's even a retractable screen that rolls down from the pillars, perfect for long, lazy—and bug-free—summer evenings. Homes in Arizona and Florida are measured including porch spaces; most homes in Minnesota aren't, but I don't understand why. A thoughtfully designed home incorporates the indoors and outdoors in a way that lets people enjoy fresh air and sunshine throughout the seasons.

FACING PAGE: The client and I designed the railings together. I love to see people get personally engaged in the creation of their homes. It helps to make a dwelling that much more personal.
Photographs courtesy of Eskuche Creative Group

"I believe a home should engage in a conversation with its surroundings—trees, sky, water, prairie, hills—and respond by adding value and beauty."

—Peter Eskuche

ABOVE & FACING PAGE: This "farmhouse meets the Hamptons" style home nestles quietly into the countryside, while the interior is surprisingly roomy. Like many people, the homeowners instinctively follow the sun throughout their daily routines; this design accommodates that. Thanks to elevated windows, natural light brightens two-story rooms on the west side without beaming directly into people's faces. The cupola up top floods the children's sitting room with light. Best of all, the stunning porch wraps completely around the living areas, jutting out just enough to take advantage of summertime breezes and to provide protected spaces in cooler months. Other favorite features: a garage that looks like a stable and geothermal heating, which saves resources.
Photographs courtesy of Eskuche Creative Group

"The home is by far my favorite design project—even the smallest, simplest spaces can be filled with personality and invested with soul."

—Peter Eskuche

ABOVE: The dwelling sits on a narrow lake lot full of towering trees, but it's flooded with natural light and personality thanks to quirky windows situated at the top of tall spaces. A playful swoop roof breaks up the line of the garage.

FACING PAGE TOP: The fun-loving, casual attitude of the owners shows in every detail, while the home itself blends wonderfully into its historical neighborhood. To make the most of stunning second-story views, we placed the cozy family room up on the second level and adjoined it with a protected terrace.

FACING PAGE BOTTOM: On many a morning the owners enjoy sunrises and leisurely breakfasts on the porch. Situated just below the balcony, it's protected from winter winds and can be warmed by a roaring fire—the ultimate in informal indoor-outdoor living.
Photographs courtesy of Eskuche Creative Group

Ever wonder what makes a home memorable? What really sets a house apart? Although invisible to the eye, the relationship between the architect and the homeowner is one of the most critical elements. Collaboration, chemistry—it is vital to the equation of success.

Knowing the clients and understanding what is important to them and the virtues that it adds to a home's aesthetic is clear. JDA Design Architects has worked with this in mind since its founding in 1992; principal John Anderson knows that his connection with the client means everything. It is imperative for strong results. And working in the land of 10,000 lakes certainly doesn't hurt the homes' appeal. The organic quality of JDA Design's work shines in the Minnesota landscape and reveals a sensitivity to the environment; the homes are infused into their surroundings and celebrate the landscapes of the Midwest and beyond.

"A successful home for us is one that reflects its surroundings, suits the needs of its owner and highlights creativity wherever possible."

—John Anderson

JDA DESIGN ARCHITECTS

RIGHT: Combining the owners' style with our own, the horse ranch features loads of heavy timber and an array of other natural materials. The selections result in a rich, warm exterior that looks even more inviting against piling snow.

PREVIOUS PAGES: A lake home in northwestern Wisconsin held special meaning for the homeowner; as a boy he grew up fishing this lake and knew he wanted a home that recaptured his childhood memories. In order to make the house fit on the site, JDA Design was forced to take down three large white pine trees, more than originally thought. To make up for this, JDA Design honored the materials by placing the logs as a central element within the living room. The pine logs were harvested by the homeowners, a process that won't soon be forgotten. Camping on the site for days, the owners peeled the bark from the logs themselves using a traditional drawknife and sent them to the timber mill to be dried in a kiln. After the logs were returned to the site, they were hoisted into place where they sit beautifully in the couple's living room as both an homage to their location and a souvenir of their laboring endeavor.

Photographs by Rau+Barber Photography

"A home should never solely represent the architect's style."

—John Anderson

RIGHT: Sunlight reveals the craftsmanship of the details. Hand-assembled structural trusses, steel gusset plates and perfectly oriented windows catch the eye.

FACING PAGE: With classic ranch style, the interior responds to its exterior surroundings. The master suite, great room and master bathroom all offer sweeping views of the 80-acre horse ranch. Transparent and bright, every room has an injection of the outdoors and offers a connection to the placid pastures beyond its walls.
Photographs by Rau+Barber Photography

"We look at neighbors like extended family. A home should increase the sense of comfort for both the homeowners and the neighborhood."

—John Anderson

ABOVE: Natural stone, heavy timber and metal roofing dominate the award-winning home. In 2005, the home received a national design award for best custom house under 3,000 square feet. The open front porch and extensive walking trails offer an interactive neighborhood feel. Glowing from within, the house gives off a look-and-see warmth to neighbors and passersby—an element that creates a sense of comfort for both the residents and the community. One glance from the street will make anyone want to step inside and join the family.
Photograph courtesy of JDA Design

FACING PAGE: During the design process, we were meticulous. We knew that a Western influence would be apparent but the finer points would need to be deliberated. It took us seven months to finally break ground—but the lengthy process paid off in the end.
Photograph by Rau+Barber Photography

LEFT: Commanding and strong, the interior offers two-story spaces with an open feel.
Photograph courtesy of JDA Design

FACING PAGE TOP: Boulder retaining walls, a jutting porch and use of heavy timber give the Minnesota home its memorable characteristics. Set on a five-acre parcel, the house aims to take advantage of as much daylight as possible by employing numerous windows and glass doors to bring the light deeper into the home.
Photograph by DW Media

FACING PAGE BOTTOM: Built on an open lot, the Minneapolis home conveys some of our trademark characteristics: plenty of rich woods and the sense of transparency.
Photograph by Rau+Barber Photography

Art means something in Minnesota. And architecture in Minnesota is far above that of other regions. Architect Steve Kleineman of SKD Architects has over 30 years of experience in commercial, governmental and residential architecture and—whichever the type of project—designs to evoke reactions as if each is a work of art. A medium-sized firm, SKD is flexible and responsive to the challenges of the rich diversity found in the Minnesota environment, work ethic, lifestyle, culture and especially, its own clients.

Architecture doesn't end with the design. Steve sees each project through from conception to construction to completion. Working with capable and knowledgeable builders is key to seeing SKD's work come to fruition— not only to realize the vision of the architect, but also that of the clients. With superior builders such as its sister company, MS&I Building Company, SKD ensures that each project is approached with equal parts of the management, skill and imagination required to give homeowners their dreams.

"Our architecture nourishes the senses. People feel elation through visual excitement as well as the touch and feel of a well-detailed and finished home."

—Steve Kleineman

SKD ARCHITECTS

"We want jaws to drop when people walk into each of our projects."

—Steve Kleineman

RIGHT: A play on form and height gives the living area artful movement and a welcoming appeal and is further enhanced by the horizontal highlights of metal and wood detailing. For a more formal appearance to the ambience, integrated wood doors can cover the television and the fireplace is easily set ablaze. With tall ceilings, rooms can often seem vast and uncomfortable, but staggered levels of ceiling height with lighting break down what could be an overwhelming sense of volume. By starting illumination at a height of nine-foot four-inches and reaching to 15 feet, the area maintains an intimate feeling.
Photograph by Jim Kruger, LandMark Photography

PREVIOUS PAGE LEFT: Carrying through the organic contemporary theme of the home, the kitchen and adjacent hearth room incorporate the four elements. Beyond the eye-catching effervescent light fixture, the stone details, integrated wood cabinetry and exquisite custom-designed metalwork anchor the space as the heart of the home while also making it a warm gathering space for family and friends.
Photograph by Jill Greer

PREVIOUS PAGE RIGHT: A Wayzata family wanted a warm, artistic, livable house. It was to have an organic, earthy feel and be a contemporary interpretation of Asian-influenced Prairie-style architecture.
Photograph by Jill Greer

"Architecture is art…and our architecture is livable art."

—Steve Kleineman

ABOVE: Even though a home on Lake Minnetonka was built over a decade ago, it hasn't lost an ounce of contemporary appeal. The home stands two stories tall, yet appears to be only one level from the exterior. Large, elegantly stretched windows and an oversized entrance help create this look. Stone and stucco make up the outside; a protective entrance extends 14 feet to accommodate arrivals during the often-snowy months of winter.
Photograph by Saari & Forrai Photography

FACING PAGE: Offices have become the sanctuary of a house. Whether the homeowner is a busy parent or a busy professional—or both—a quiet place is always welcome. Because of its respite nature, seamless planning reinforces the room's calming effect. Motorized shades and warm lighting assist in making certain just the right amount of brightness is allowed. Even bookshelves are artful and peaceful in their composition. Symmetry, cozy materials, spaces for art, books and even rest; the cabinetry and shelving nestles around a u-shaped work area with a wireless desk arrangement for the perfect environment.
Photographs by Jill Greer

"Timelessness is essential to good architecture."

—Steve Kleineman

LEFT: This is the fourth house we have designed for the clients. As the couple has matured, their tastes have changed from wanting edgier modern looks to preferring modern interpretations of traditional styles. Richness is conveyed, but reinterpreted, in the design and materials of the translucent dome, repeated circular forms and spaces, and details of grandeur.
Photograph by Jill Greer

FACING PAGE: Particularly important to the couple was designing the home for larger-scale entertaining—personal and charitable—as well as private living which was artfully and harmoniously achieved by separating the spaces with the central spiral staircase.
Top photograph by Steve Kleineman
Bottom photograph by Jill Greer

"We are a design-oriented, design-sensitive and design-focused firm. We continually influence the way people live, work and play."

—Steve Kleineman

ABOVE: The owners wanted a contemporary and rich waterfront environment to live in, which is not to be understated. They appreciate the finer things and take notice of the details, but also wanted to want to stay home. Just off of the master suite, the terrace gives the homeowners their own private virtual ship deck from which they view and experience the beauty of Lake Minnetonka.

FACING PAGE: The site is on a large, open bay with plenty of sailboats and activity, visible from the entire lake side of the home. To further marry the structure with the site, the home was designed with nautical elements from the circular windows, to the bowed sailing-inspired rails, to the wood and metal bridge. *Photographs by Karen Melvin*

Bruckelmyer Brothers LLC, page 67

Cates Fine Homes, page 77

the structure

chapter two

Hendel Homes, page 87

John Kraemer and Sons Inc., page 97

MS&I Building Company, page 107

There is no guesswork with Bruckelmyer Brothers—what you see is what you get. The employee-based firm brings high quality craftsmanship and years of construction management experience, which is evident in every project.

After being employed in the construction industry for nearly 10 years, brothers Dennis and Ed began the company in 1988, focusing on remodeling, decks, roofing, garages and subcontracting. Their portfolio expanded in 1992, building the first full custom home and later in 2000 when the custom cabinetry shop opened. Bruckelmyer Brothers now offers interior design, cabinetry, custom closets, restoration mouldings, timber work and commercial construction services. The Bruckelmyer team collaborates with northern Minnesota's finest architects and pursues top-notch systems for every project. Energy efficient construction methods and materials hold high priority, including insulated concrete forms, air-tight construction, triple-pane windows and doors, as well as geothermal heating and cooling. Growing steadily since its beginnings, the firm has clearly gained the high opinion of Minnesotans; word of mouth has been its primary means of developing.

"When you do good work, people talk about it. We know that our reputation is on the line with each project."

—Dennis Bruckelmyer

BRUCKELMYER BROTHERS LLC

ABOVE & FACING PAGE: Quiet and secluded, an Island Lake home sits on a private bay with 12 acres of surrounding land. Wood banding, genuine stone veneer and metalwork railing add character to the isolated house; the handcrafted timbers come from reclaimed Douglas fir, originally from an old building. To add function to form, we installed a geothermal heating system to give an efficient means of warming the home.

PREVIOUS PAGES: Overlooking Lake Superior, the home we built has a strong cedar exterior, custom beam work and pavilion for an outdoors-loving family. Native split fieldstone provides a rustic look and is often harvested from the farms of northern Minnesota, collected from fields when clearing and piled in the corners of their land. The interior of the home celebrates its location on the great lake; the bridge over the entryway features an antique wheel of a ship from the early 20th century.

Photographs courtesy of Bruckelmyer Brothers

LEFT: Dark stucco, Rumford-style fireplaces, natural Brynmawr stone and recycled composite slate roofing give the home Old World charm while providing space for the most modern items. A 60-by-40 foot finished, matching and heated garage building holds the homeowners' pontoon and watercraft—must haves for lake living—plus two attached garages for the family vehicles.

Photograph courtesy of Bruckelmyer Brothers

"We love working with wood. It represents the appeal of northern Minnesota and allows our talented employees to really show their skills."

—Ed Bruckelmyer

LEFT: A masculine den has become a relaxation area for the man of the house. The Rumford-style fireplace sits back to back with a screened porch, featuring custom woodwork on both sides. A carefully painted rendition of Island Lake appears on the ceiling; crafted detail gives the room its character.

FACING PAGE TOP: Since the Island Lake residents love to entertain, it's no surprise that their kitchen features granite countertops, custom cabinetry and a design fit to accommodate any gathering. The home also has a full bar with pressed-tin ceilings, capturing the quality of old-fashion pubs.

FACING PAGE BOTTOM: We put a variety of species to work in order to create the perfect room; wood detailing appears in almost every corner of the home. A pillar pediment uses 130 miters in its top section alone while a bathroom shows off the rich color of timber in a sink stand.

Photographs courtesy of Bruckelmyer Brothers

"With triple-digit summers and extreme negative-number winters, Minnesota weather is a great test of our work. Year after year, it proves more than reliable."

—Ed Bruckelmyer

ABOVE: Sitting in a wooded area in Bristolwood, the home belongs to an engineer and his wife—we built the home and customized every detail to fit their lifestyle. She was an integral part of interior design and made sure every element suited the family's taste. Entertaining is a big part of their lives, and each room keeps this in mind with thoughtful layouts. While the adults primarily stay on the ground floor, the two young daughters spend a good deal of their time in the lower level, which offers a home theater and matching bedroom suites.

FACING PAGE: The custom cherry interior and Marvin windows give the home a classic look. The front door hints to the family's history, both hailing from Texas. The design embraces the family's lives by bringing an aspect of their personalities into each space.
Photographs courtesy of Bruckelmyer Brothers

Integrity. Craftsmanship. Family. These are the qualities that define Cates Fine Homes. Located in Stillwater, Minnesota, Cates brings together the best elements to create custom homes.

Started by Judd Cates in 1970, the operation has always been a family affair. Drawing from his life-long experience, Judd has taught his three children the importance of first-rate work. Instilling a strong work ethic, Judd began exposing Jay, Jennifer and Jeff to job sites at young ages. Jay developed his natural talents as a leader and has taken the family forward since assuming his role as a contractor. Jennifer is the voice of Cates, taking charge of communications and facilitating smooth day-to-day functions. With a business degree and CPA background, Jennifer carries the responsibility of financial management as well. The youngest brother, Jeff, works as project manager with the guiding philosophy that each home is a personal venture—every detail counts.

Cates brings together the Midwest's finest architects, designers and craftsmen to create stunning homes. Homeowners feel comforted by the family's passion for their work and solid record that began with Judd Cates' vision.

"Trust your builder and the team they've put together. They have nothing but the homeowners' best interest at heart."

—Jeff Cates

CATES FINE HOMES

ABOVE: Jackson Meadows is a progressive home development that promotes community and conservation, attracting worldwide attention for its sophisticated and responsive architecture and planning. Signature white exteriors, stunning metal roofs and keen design show off unique homes from David Salmela.
Photograph by Kelly Walker

FACING PAGE: The Scandinavian farmhouse-style metal roofing and prairie setting serve as trademarks for Jackson Meadow, the 2005 AIA recipient of the Honor Award for Regional and Urban Design. Throughout the residence, the clean use of white and glass stands out, crisp and inviting.
Photographs by Robin Culbreath

PREVIOUS PAGE LEFT: Native to the state, Chilton stone makes up a striking wood-burning fireplace for a lake home. Built as a retreat for an urban dweller, the home shows off exposed glu-lam structural beams on an arched tongue-and-groove fir ceiling.
Photograph by Kelly Walker

PREVIOUS PAGE RIGHT: Our favorite feature of the home is its galvalume curved roof, defining the retreat's space among its surroundings. The metal bump-out reveals a shower with glass block accents. Every detail of the home remains in harmony with the heavily wooded environment.
Photograph by Kelly Walker

"Experience matters in the homebuilding industry. And we've been doing this for nearly 40 years."

—Judd Cates

ABOVE & FACING PAGE: We built a Tuscan-inspired home after a couple went through a devastating fire with their longtime residence. The new dwelling became immeasurably important after losing so much. Endeared immediately, the homeowners loved the elements with European warmth: cedar shake roof, ledged windows with large shutters, dark chocolate-hued pillars, stucco and stone.
Photographs by Robert Bourdaghs

"Don't compromise on features that may be difficult to change in the future, like the footprint of the home, use of in-floor heat and window design. A good builder accommodates requests that reflect long-term decisions."

—Jennifer Cates Peterson

RIGHT & FACING PAGE: The couple who commissioned us to build a new home after losing theirs in a fire found a mantel that resembled their previous one. Symbolizing what they had lost, the mantel became an important representation of rebuilding their lives. Consequently, it was paramount in designing the room, retrofitted perfectly to coordinate with the cork checkerboard floor. The master bathroom has added features that show an attention to detail, like the carefully crafted wall sconces and the windows above the vanity that welcome in light.
Photographs by Robert Bourdaghs

"If an architect can draw it, we can build it."

—Jay Cates

LEFT: A stand-out exterior color accents the dramatic roof lines of a Prairie-style home. Conservation-minded home sites add touches like wild flowers, which really create a strong sense of location.

FACING PAGE: Within the home, the theme of conservation and green principles continues. Milled from Douglas fir shelves that once lined the interior of a nearby Montgomery Ward storage facility, the flooring artfully contrasts details of the décor, like the orange shade and vivid chair coverings.
Photographs by Robert Bourdaghs

You can't hide passion—so it's no secret that Rick Hendel absolutely loves what he does. Beginning his career as a carpenter, Rick worked his way up to operating a unique building company, gaining skill and experience along the way. Licensed nearly a decade ago, Hendel Homes now creates some of Minnesota's most distinct residences, conjuring up the estates of Europe's Old World.

Perhaps the most telling characteristic of a Hendel home is the fact that it could belong to any region of the world. The architecture does not give away its Minnesota roots but instead reveals the ability to integrate a variety of styles and movements into one home—seemingly without effort. Structures of Tuscany, England and France show their influence in a Hendel home, giving Midwesterners the perfect opportunity to enjoy some of the world's foremost architecture together with the comfort and convenience of the latest in innovative features.

"My passion in life is to bring back architectural concepts from history and incorporate them into today's new spaces, making them distinctive and more beautiful than ever."

—Rick Hendel

HENDEL HOMES

"If your designer or builder isn't ready to put their heart and soul into a project, keep looking. They should care about every detail."

—Rick Hendel

ABOVE: The hearth room features 14-foot doors, allowing light from all sides to show off beautifully reclaimed terracotta flooring and grand vaulted ceilings. Adjacent to the kitchen's breakfast area, the room also sits above a bistro patio, offering ideal entertaining possibilities.

FACING PAGE: An arched, burl wood entryway and a spectacular chandelier constructed with metalwork from Europe welcomes guests to the great room, which sits just beyond with a view of the lake.

PREVIOUS PAGES: After a family lost their home in a devastating fire, they wanted to rebuild the house with a feeling of expansion and growth. Set on four acres and laid out to take advantage of views of the wooded hillside and lake beyond, the home is designed with a nod to the look of Old World homes, appearing as if additions have taken place over the years. An arched drive-under breezeway connects the nanny's quarters to the primary living space.
Photographs by John Reed Forsman Photography

ABOVE & LEFT: We created a kitchen to fit with the home's warmth and still provide ample space for guests. Custom-designed cabinetry using various wood finishes gives it a sense of classic charm. A butcher-block top with slots to hold a complete knife set, concealed refrigerator, cast-stone hood and hidden dishwasher give the home cook function and form. An adjacent butler's pantry provides storage and preparation space for dinner parties and gatherings. With most families, the kitchen becomes the main hangout. Practical access lets the traffic flow easily in this large home, with three entries into the space.

FACING PAGE: Careful craftsmanship and a great deal of time went into the dining room. We used plaster for the cove ceiling, custom ironwork and hand-scraped flooring to achieve the look we wanted.

Photographs by John Reed Forsman Photography

"The mark of a timeless home is its ability to fit into any region; its personality should extend beyond Minnesota."

—Rick Hendel

ABOVE: A back view of the home overlooking the lake continues architectural features of stone, ironwork and arches.

FACING PAGE: The Mediterranean-style wine cellar sits below the tower-like extension. Old stone beams, rich woodwork and crafted tiles give the appearance of an underground vault from France or Italy in the 18th century. As part owners of a California vineyard, the homeowners place a great deal of value on the humidity-controlled cellar. An outdoor room sits on the lower level of the rear elevations. Below the hearth room, the space is screened in to enjoy the views of the lake but still remains connected to the interior. A 12-foot door gives residents the option of opening up the room or secluding it from the rest of the house. A stone fireplace, cooking grill, copper-top island and wire-brush cedar cabinetry make this an ideal setting for indoor-outdoor entertaining and gives the room a memorable look that maintains the feel of the home.

Photographs by John Reed Forsman Photography

"Traveling has been a huge influence on my work. It's a great resource for inspiration."

—Rick Hendel

ABOVE & RIGHT: Our careful selection of materials makes a big difference in a project's results. Reclaimed beams, exotic burl wood veneers, crotch-cut mahogany and sapeli veneer together with a marble hearth offer the office richness, warmth and a strong furniture quality, as opposed to straightforward cabinets. Outside, wood beams and a variety of Indian Creek stone were meticulously chosen for a look that would have existed long ago. We used 3,000-pound stones for the posts, cut them down, and slid them into the foundation to give a weathered appearance.
Photographs by Jim Mims Photography

FACING PAGE TOP: Walnut floors get their appeal from our technique; we burned the wood for a French bleed before sanding them back to give a smooth surface. The checkered butcher-block top, made of walnut and maple, accents the room and gives rich details to the kitchen.
Photograph by Michael Zaccardi Photography

FACING PAGE BOTTOM: For a French-style home, we used large quantities of cast stone and limestone to create an authentic feel. Copper gutters, fully functional shutters and a custom garage door, which appears to swing open, give the home a realistic, elegant European flavor. The front door makes a strong case for the home's stature, revealing quality and craftsmanship as people pass through the threshold.
Photograph by Michael Zaccardi Photography

With the amount of hard work and long hours required in the home-building industry, only the people who love it stick with it. The family behind John Kraemer and Sons is a shining example of that; the family puts every ounce of fire into what they do. But prospective homebuyers don't have to take their word for it—the work speaks for itself.

John Kraemer and Sons, founded by Gary Kraemer and his late father John in 1978, has been the Parade of Homes Dream Home Builder, won the Builder of the Year Award and received the Reggie Award of Excellence multiple times, as well as the People's Choice Award. John's hard work and dedication put a face with the American dream. He grew up on a farm, served his country and worked for the then-booming Ford Company. But what began as a side job in the early 1950s really captured his attention and eventually turned into the family's greatest asset: He began building and renovating homes. John's passion has trickled down through the family. Gary's two oldest sons, John and Jeff, have joined the team, adding their natural gifts and passion for business and construction. Often chosen by the state's finest architects, the builders use a tight network of hand-picked craftsmen to implement the architect and homeowner's vision, ensuring consistency and trust. Proven by a 30-year-long record of stunning homes, the Kraemer approach to building is as successful as it is solid.

"We believe in Aristotle's notion that 'We are what we repeatedly do. Excellence, then, is not an act but a habit.' This philosophy sums up our work approach."

—Gary Kraemer

JOHN KRAEMER AND SONS INC.

ABOVE: An indoor pool can maintain all of the virtues of its outdoor counterpart. Neon lighting, fiber optic star patterns and the exact layout of the northern sky give swimmers the distinct feeling of swimming under the night's heavens. A cloud machine plus the illusions of twinkling and shooting stars make the experience complete—even Galileo would be fooled. And an automatic cover adds a touch of sensibility and safety.
Photograph by Jon Huelskamp, LandMark Photography

FACING PAGE: Employing the world's best craftsmen during the building process, we chose a company in California to create the custom iron railing and shipped it to Minnesota for installation. Ornate detailing accents the treads and risers of the marble stairways.
Photograph by Jim Kruger, LandMark Photography

PREVIOUS PAGES: A heavy reliance on word-of-mouth attests to the fact that the work speaks for itself. One view of a home on Lake Minnetonka says it all, revealing impressive use of hand-crafted cast Indiana limestone.
Photograph by Jon Huelskamp, LandMark Photography

"Our mission is to build and renovate the finest homes in the country. All of our energy is focused on this. Homeowners should embrace this separation of church and state, so to speak. Let architects design and builders build—that's the path to the best results."

—Gary Kraemer

RIGHT: Sight lines are undoubtedly important when building within vibrant natural surroundings. Minnesota has some of the country's most breathtaking scenery, so when building a home that sits near a lake or other natural setting, consider a window-after-window design to bring the outdoors into the home.
Photograph by Jon Huelskamp, LandMark Photography

"Our commitment to excellence extends to every detail."

—John Kraemer

ABOVE: A Prairie-style design on White Bear Lake serves as a perfect venue to show off keen landscaping, as well as reveal a breadth of diversity.

FACING PAGE TOP: Renovations are a large part of the Kraemer business and can provide a new feel to any home. We transformed an existing storage area behind the home's bar into a wine room. Holding roughly 250 bottles, the room was an exciting change and continues to promote entertaining and family gatherings within the residence.

FACING PAGE BOTTOM: Both traditional and modern versions of libraries seem to have one thing in common: They feature a blend of rich woods. For a knotty pine library, hand-scraped white oak flooring from a Chicago-based company was used.

Photographs by Jim Kruger, LandMark Photography

"We love building in a variety of styles. Our favorite home is the one we're working on."

—Gary Kraemer

ABOVE: A cedar roof, cedar shake siding, enormous lush trees and a meticulous exterior make the Lake Minnetonka home appear like a postcard snapshot.
Photograph by Jim Kruger, LandMark Photography

FACING PAGE: It's all about the details. From two-and-a-half-inch double-thick granite countertops to custom-painted tapestry murals, to reclaimed timber beams and natural stone, the work stands up to even the most scrutinizing eye.
Photographs by Jon Huelskamp, LandMark Photography

What's the best way to bring imagination and skill together in a company environment? Keen management. For a building company to reach its potential, imagination, skill and management have to work together in perfect balance. In an effort to successfully realize this philosophy, MS&I Building Company was developed in 2000 by Steve Kleineman of SKD Architects, a firm that believes in the abilities of Dan Mulrennan and Joe Janetka to carry out the credo. Dan, Joe and Steve have been in the business of building and designing for most of their lives. The talented partners use their unique strengths to work together and maintain the architectural integrity while being mindful of the budget and building methods. Using a proven network of tradespeople, artisans and other architects on occasion, MS&I consistently surpasses its clients' expectations. And likewise, clients see how well MS&I's approach works, emphasizing their personal enjoyment of both the process and the end results.

"We keep management, skill and imagination at the forefront of our working philosophy."

—Dan Mulrennan

MS&I BUILDING COMPANY

"We are very sensitive to the built form and thrive on our combined passions of architecture and building. One does not happen successfully without the other."

—Dan Mulrennan

ABOVE & FACING PAGE: Entertaining is not just for having large gatherings; the family—alone—should enjoy the rooms as well. For the lower-level remodeling of a home, our task was like building a ship in a bottle—detail was extraordinary with minimal access.
Photographs by Jill Greer

PREVIOUS PAGES: When art-loving homeowners wanted to reflect their interests in a home, we built a space that felt like an art gallery. Whether a painting, a sculpture or a piece of furniture, each item is displayed to highlight its beauty, taking advantage of the natural light that pours through the windows. Emphasizing aesthetics, privacy and efficiency, the plans favored a vertical design to fit within the confines of a site with multiple restrictions.
Photographs by Saari & Forrai Photography

CAST

BUILDER   DAN MULRENNAN
ARCHITECT   STEVE KLEINEMAN
SITE SUPERVISOR JOE JANETKA

ABOVE: Just beyond the informal eating area lies a formal dining room, both showing extensive detail. Used together, the two spaces are perfect for large families or entertaining. A butler pantry off to the side provides plenty of storage for culinary goods and an area for food preparation out of the view of guests.

FACING PAGE: We tune in to the style of the architect. Each has a distinct finesse, seen in the master suite of a Minnetonka home. The bathroom and bedroom bring together Asian influences as well as contemporary and traditional elements while providing the owner with a serene retreat.
Photographs by Jill Greer

"We don't leave any detail unresolved."

—Dan Mulrennan

LEFT: The outdoors are just as important as the indoors, which is why we integrate the two. Minnesota experiences all four seasons but is best known for its extremely cold and snowy winters. This home was built to celebrate the warmer months with access to the outdoor recreational areas by way of both the upper and lower levels.

FACING PAGE TOP: Just after moving into their new home, the clients expressed their delight with the new master suite by comparing it to waking up in a five-star hotel every morning. From their vantage point, they are able to enjoy a lovely view...or the covered terrace only feet away through a sliding glass door—a Minnesota lanai.

FACING PAGE BOTTOM: Described as an oasis, the master bathroom features walnut custom cabinetry, stone floors, marble countertops and a glass-encased steam shower. Designer lighting and plumbing fixtures work with the architectural details to create an aesthetic and soothing spa-like environment.
Photographs by Jill Greer

"Our materials reflect nature and what it offers. Stone, wood, marble, glass and metal—uniquely combined—are the elements that anchor our homes."

—Dan Mulrennan

ABOVE: The hearth room's folding glass doors allow a nearly seamless transition to the covered terrace. Additionally, the motorized screens can defend them against the Minnesota mosquitoes when lowered and allow outdoor living to extend well into the evening hours. Beyond the covered terrace and past the pool sits an MS&I-built playhouse, constructed and designed for charity. The artistry and craftsmanship is so noteworthy that even a couple without young children found it irresistible.

FACING PAGE: From the pool deck, the covered terrace and hearth room await. The window of the master bedroom sits just off to the right, accessed by a sliding glass door, making the terrace ideal for relaxing before bed or enjoying coffee in the morning. Built to make sense, each room complements the surrounding spaces.
Photographs by Jill Greer

"A well-compiled team gets their inspiration from one another. Our firm's creativity thrives on the input of each member."

—Steven Streeter

elements of structure

chapter three

Never underestimate the power of collaboration. The efforts of Charles R. Stinson Architects and Streeter & Associates have resulted in some of Minnesota's most beautiful homes. Working closely together for more than 20 years, the two firms hold the clients' vision as their number one objective.

When the philosophical ideas of an architect like Charles Stinson meet the hardworking determination of a builder like Streeter & Associates, the results never fail to impress. Aware, smart and always evolving, the two teams put 100 percent into their projects, whether it be an intimate remodel or a massive new construction. Charles brings an organic, holistic approach to the table, which offers a distinct Stinson style. Perfectly crafted elements interact: Light, space and an array of lines come to the forefront. With Streeter & Associates' two decades of experience the combination is ideal. Steven, Kevin, Donald and Justin make up the family team that started the firm. With solid roots in the western Minnesota countryside, they maintain traditional values that place people first. Their commitment to the craft plus their efforts of co-creation with Charles R. Stinson Architects have resulted in some of the state's most recognizable homes.

CHARLES R. STINSON ARCHITECTS | STREETER & ASSOCIATES

"Urban sites, privacy and panoramic views don't have to be mutually exclusive."

—Kevin Streeter

ABOVE & FACING PAGE: For a home that overlooks the water, we wanted to keep an open floorplan with clear sightlines. Sitting area, entertainment space and kitchen all blend with one another, designed with clean lines that extend throughout the rooms. We took great care with the lighting and fenestration; the fenestration lines up to allow for clear views of both the water and the city. The Valcucine kitchen offers unmatched elegance and luxury, featuring warm green hues that play against the outdoor views. Landscape design by Coen + Partners.

PREVIOUS PAGES: The urban site now makes up what was once three separate lots. The homeowners, relocating from Belgium, wanted to take advantage of the ability to have a private setting with plenty of space within the city. Simple floating structures use clean limestone boulders in combination with a variety of rich textures. We worked closely with Coen + Partners for the careful integration of landscape—an element critical to the home's appeal.
Photographs by Peter Bastianelli-Kerze

"There's no reason a home can't look and feel as luxurious as an upscale hotel."

—Justin Streeter

ABOVE: Built in the same vein as a boutique hotel, the master bathroom features all of the lavish comforts that a retreat would offer. While showering, the homeowners can look out and see the city. This translucency, mixed with sleek elements like a Corian tub, gives the space a modern simplicity. Landscape design by Coen + Partners.
Photograph by Peter Bastianelli-Kerze

FACING PAGE: Slated to sit on Cedar Lake in the Twin Cities, a phase-two home features an open, all-glass design. Glass walkways link deck space on the second floor with the yoga room and guesthouse. With no roads nearby, the home has views of lush Minnesota meadows. Landscape design by Coen + Partners.
Top rendering by Charles R. Stinson Architects
Bottom rendering by Coen + Partners

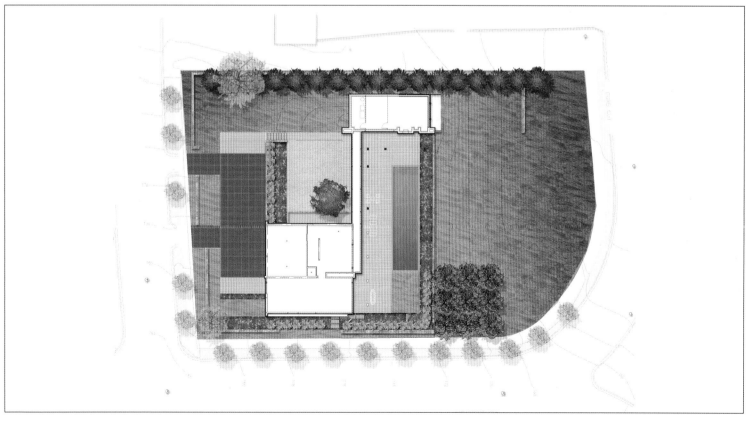

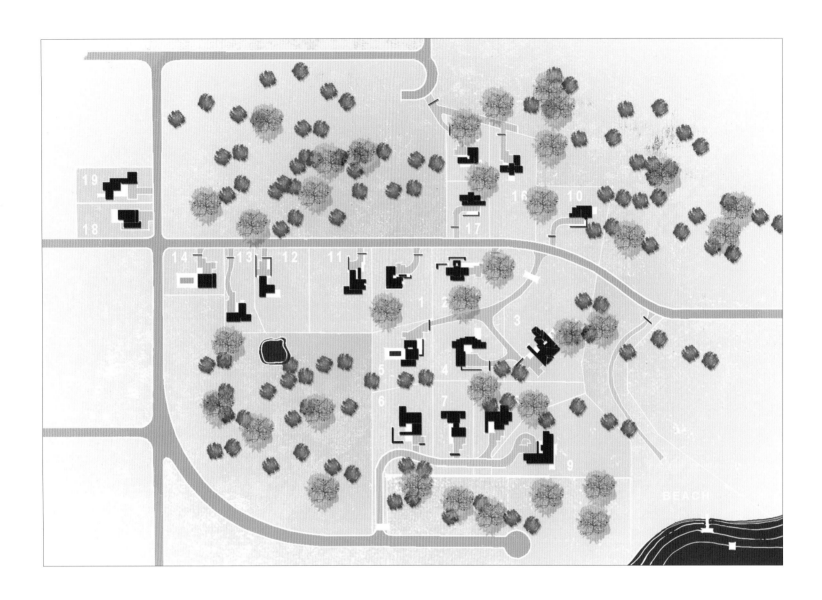

"Nothing gives a home instant authenticity like a site enveloped by mature trees."

—Donald Streeter

ABOVE: Ted and Kathy DeLancey helped save a Chanhassen neighborhood, putting our companies to work on the design and development side. Fifteen years ago, the couple pushed to grow the area without any harm to the environment, letting the homes sit among nature's design. Jumping from nine to 19 lots, the neighborhood features serene houses; a screened-in porch and shared access to Lotus Lake keep the family connected to their preserved environment. Landscape design by Coen + Partners.
Photograph by Peter Bastianelli-Kerze

FACING PAGE: Formerly a day camp, lots one through nine—Phase I of this Lotus Lake architectural community—had been originally planted with trees by Ted Delancey's father, which has created a warm, wooded effect. Oak and maple trees fill the oversized lots, giving a tucked-away sense to the homes. The neighborhood however, remains close to schools, parks and all of the city's offerings. Chosen as one of the best cities to live, Chanhassen is a beautifully preserved piece of the Midwest. Landscape design by Coen + Partners.
Illustration by Charles R. Stinson Architects
Rendering by Coen + Partners

"Every aspect of a home should be a unique expression of its inhabitants."

—Charles R. Stinson

ABOVE: A couple who now lives in the Chanhassen neighborhood fell in love with our work immediately. Since we built all of the homes within the development, this was a huge compliment to the work we do. With precision and detail, we designed and built a house to match the couple's lifestyle. Landscape design by Coen + Partners.

FACING PAGE: Whether we're working with a pianist who conducts lessons in the home or a Chicago couple that spends a good deal of time in the city, we create homes that have creative energy and nurture the people who live within them. Landscape design by Coen + Partners.
Photographs by Peter Bastianelli-Kerze

ABOVE: For a young professional couple from India with busy schedules, we crafted a loft-style treehouse that reflects their roots. The home brings warmth and comfort to an efficient, urban design. Landscape design by Coen + Partners.

FACING PAGE: To properly build a home, we need to be there full-time. Site supervision is the only way to ensure that we achieve the perfect customized results. When the couple needed space for their concert organ and extensive art collection, we created a home that reflects their passions. We never forget that we're not just building a house; we're building a dream home. Landscape design by Coen + Partners.
Photographs by Peter Bastianelli-Kerze

Big Wood Timber Frames, Inc.

St. Paul, Minnesota

"It's important that homes reflect their geography. We use materials that speak about the region."

—Dave LePage

ABOVE & FACING PAGE: The pioneers of the upper Midwest referred to the majestic Mississippi River Valley as "Big Wood Country." A wealth of tall straight timber lent itself to the homesteads and barns of the settlers, which continue to anchor the architecture of our region. We carry the same tradition of hard labor and craftsmanship to work everyday, with a mission to transform the inherent energy of historic materials into new and wonderful forms. Twenty-inch pine floorboards and hand-hewn timbers abound.
Above photographs courtesy of Nor-Son, Inc.
Facing page photograph by Hammer Photography

"Using reclaimed materials allows our clients to add a sustainable element to their project; from timber trusses and skipped planed boards on the great room ceiling, down to the hand-scraped hardwood floor in the kitchen."

—Mike Nicklaus

ABOVE: Timber Frame construction uses a basic engineering premise with beautiful results. The method relies on an effective system of vertical and horizontal timber, held together with a coordination of specialty joinery and wooden pegs. Tie beams, rafters and ridges are some of the fundamental elements that give the structure both its strength and charm. This construction creates the most welcoming environments.
Above left photograph by Hammer Photography
Above right photograph courtesy of Nor-Son, Inc.

FACING PAGE: Because we focus on reclaimed timber, we work with demolition contractors to carefully salvage warehouse and barn materials for structural and decorative reuse. Most of our salvaged materials originate from buildings of the early to late 1800s. These old beams and planks, covered with ax marks, peg holes and nail blemishes, carry the history of the buildings and the craftsmen who built them.
Photographs by Hammer Photography

"We build homes to fit
the environment and suit
the homeowners' aesthetic,
lifestyle, wants and needs."

—Dave LePage

RIGHT & FACING PAGE: Our craftsmen also produce structural and non-structural trusses, beam ceilings, entryways and porches to enhance the beauty of conventional stick-frame homes and commercial buildings. We stock 1,000,000 board feet of inventory, enabling our clients to choose from a vast army of timber types and surface options. We pride ourselves on the ability to aid architects and homeowners in designing one-of-a-kind timber detailing. We create a solid rustic or refined charm, which endures the test of time.

Photographs by Hammer Photography

"At the heart of it, we build green. Our use of regional reclaimed materials is a good fit in today's homebuilding environment."

—Mike Nicklaus

ABOVE & FACING PAGE: Our timber frames offer an interior space that would make anyone feel right at home. But our designs have brains as well as beauty. We combine rich, organic timber with modern energy-efficient panels to create a timeless look.
Photographs by Hammer Photography

WD FLOORING DESIGN

"Operating for sustainability is a sentiment we don't take lightly."

—Peter Connor

ABOVE: Contrary to popular belief, American forest growth exceeds harvest by almost 50 percent. And because we've been in the industry for more than a century, we know that protecting this statistic is critical. Located in Wisconsin, our timberland consists of sustainable forests; we use a rotating, 40,000-acre stock.
Photograph courtesy of WD Flooring

FACING PAGE: Contrast has a powerful effect on a space. To offset the rift white oak on the walls of a home designed by Domain Architecture, we used dark walnut on the floor as well as for the island paneling.
Photograph by Gallop Studio

"Diversity of species and product choices—that's our concentration."

—Peter Connor

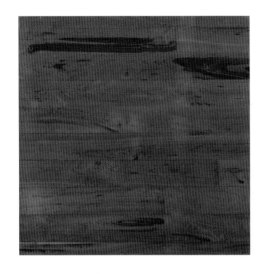

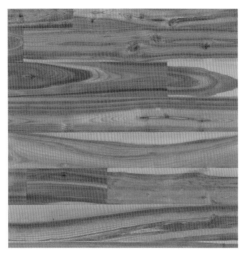

ABOVE: Conservation grade™ samples display our species diversity. We can accommodate any design effort, which is precisely why we developed proprietary grades.
Photographs courtesy of WD Flooring

FACING PAGE TOP: Our conservation grade™ maple gives a warm feel to a modern loft concept in the Bridgewater Condominiums in Minneapolis.
Photograph by Gallop Studio

FACING PAGE BOTTOM: For an office setting, we took an unexpected cue from the planks of a ship deck. Multiple species come together to create the bold statement: stained ebony ash and pickled white maple make up the flooring.
Photograph by Gallop Studio

RIGHT: FSC™ maple adds to the transparent design of a Charles Stinson stairwell.
Photograph courtesy of Charles R. Stinson Architects

FACING PAGE TOP: When we built an FSC™-certified home that required 100-percent eco-friendly materials, we explored all of our options. An FSC™ conservation grade™ floor conveys all of the advantages of a traditional hard maple floor but has a modern edge to it. The duality of classic versus contemporary is clear.
Photograph courtesy of Charles R. Stinson Architects

FACING PAGE BOTTOM: A green house doesn't have to sacrifice elegance. And we helped prove it with a Keith Waters and Associates Ideas home, rated by Minnesota Green Star. Traditional with all modern updates, the rooms use FSC™ conservation grade™ flooring in red birch.
Photographs by LandMark Photography

"W.D. Connor led in the concept of sustainable forestry in the early 20th century. We're just carrying on the tradition."

—Peter Connor

ABOVE: Without the walnut floors and clean woodwork, the room of a private residence would have a completely different feel. Our work offers simple elegance.

FACING PAGE: In the MacPhail Music School's great hall, we worked with James Dayton Designs. Our goal was to frame the room without overshadowing the performance area. Edge grain maple sets off the Douglas fir paneling. The floor shows clean lines with the wood grain running tangential to the face, minimizing any possible figuring.
Photographs by Gallop Studio

ACCENT ORNAMENTAL IRON CO.

Cambridge, Minnesota

"Ironwork is a trade, comprised of skill and art. Homeowners should always ask what artistic options they have and communicate their distinct taste—ironworkers can do some amazing work."

—Michael Stylski

ABOVE & FACING PAGE: A homeowner had picked out very specific photographs of ironwork that resembled mangroves for us to work with during the construction of a house built by Mihm Custom Homes. Beautiful as it was, the design didn't follow Minnesota's building codes for safety, which state that a four-inch sphere cannot pass through the railing. A solution to the problem satisfied both the technical aspect of the project and gave the client an end result that he couldn't have been happier with, proving that challenges are catalysts for creativity. The final product fits perfectly with the marshy surroundings of the home, sculpted in a tree branch pattern and embossed to look nearly identical to tree bark. Finished in a durable, powder coat finish, the railing gets more compliments than any other exterior feature on the home.
Photographs by Shawn Michienzi

"People usually know what style they like, whether it's contemporary, Victorian, modern or industrial. The choices are endless. It's very rewarding to help them hone in on the perfect match."

—Kelly Olene-Stylski

ABOVE: Featured in a contemporary Parade Home built by Accent Homes, the chain iron railing required careful craftsmanship. Using 27 opposing revolutions to twist the iron pieces, each six-foot segment took about an hour to create. This particular project began as simple stainless cable railing until a trip to our extensive showroom changed the client's mind.
Photographs courtesy of Accent Homes

FACING PAGE: Sponsored by the National Ornamental & Miscellaneous Metals Association, the International Metalcraft Competition awarded our stair railing—within a Mihm custom home—for outstanding interior railing. Laborious and rewarding, the stair railing took approximately 560 man hours to craft. For us, winning a top honor has special meaning. It not only acknowledges our hard work, it also represents a voice of approval from industry peers.
Photograph by Shawn Michienzi

"Results reveal the passion of a craftsman. With a father in the same trade, I've been doing this work since I was seven years old; and I think my results show just how much I love it."

—Michael Stylski

ABOVE & FACING PAGE: Working with Edina craftsman and contractor John Burch, we specially built a stair railing for an enclosed space. The use of smaller materials became crucial in order to keep the structure from overwhelming the contained area. The railing was constructed to fit the alder wood cap, mastering cohesion to give the work a seamless look. Bolted in two spots and epoxy-bonded into place, the staircase shows off detailed, Old World workmanship without the grandeur of an ostentatious foyer.
Photographs by Shawn Michienzi

JOHNSTON MASONRY

Duluth, Minnesota

"We aren't just concerned with getting the job done; working with owners, builders and architects as a team is critical to success."

—Ken Johnston

ABOVE: No detail goes unnoticed. And a Rumford-style fireplace in a Bruckelmyer Brothers home is the perfect example of that. By using a mixture of a large cast-stone mantel and the same mosaic patterns that make up the home's exterior, we created the perfect 48-inch fireplace for this lake home. Black firebrick was used in place of the typical yellow-toned variety, making a huge difference in the project's appearance.

FACING PAGE: Located on Island Lake near Duluth, a project called for our attention from the early bid-and-design stage. By coming in and providing a budget analysis, we saved the homeowner tens of thousands of dollars on the overall cost. They had chosen a stone that was less than ideal; we provided the necessary information for them to make a wiser decision. In the end, the installment was efficient and the stone worked perfectly with their design. The project demonstrates our ability to deliver the full package: happy homeowners, objective craftsmanship and cost control. *Photographs courtesy of Bruckelmyer Brothers*

"Old World masonry plus new technology equals unmatched quality."

—Ken Johnston

TOP: When we worked on the home of a well known Minneapolis architect, our team rose to the occasion. Expectations were high, making the project a bit more challenging. We created the project with all natural stone and used the skills of our master stone masons to do the carving—the homeowner was more than pleased.

MIDDLE: A Duluth area, dry-stacked wall shows off the talent of our master stone masons. Completing several each year, our team is called on, by both architects and homeowners, to produce the highest quality freestanding and retaining walls.

BOTTOM: Size isn't everything—small projects can leave just as much of an impression as large ones. And a finely detailed fireplace shows that, from the herringbone firebox made with thin soapstone firebrick, to the stainless steel mantel supports with large hand-carved stone pieces. Practical and easy on the eyes, the fireplace is a memorable addition to the home.

FACING PAGE: We maintain lasting, loyal relationships with builders; Anderson Hammock of Superior, Wisconsin, has worked with us for years. For a large project in the northern area of the state, we collaborated for over a year to create stand-out stone work. Far from an average job, the home required a local field stone that we handpicked and cleaned—over 150 tons total. We were able to control the sizes, fit and color to achieve the precise vision. Total, the results yielded a crafted exterior veneer, four large fireplaces, a full-stone driveway, a stone-front garage and a number of retaining walls and walkways.

Photographs by Johnston Masonry

"Our reputation is one of our strongest assets."

—Ken Johnston

ABOVE LEFT: Homeowners will often ask us to design and build a piece without seeing any preliminary drawings or pictures—they have full confidence in us and love surprises. With these circumstances, we crafted a fireplace that absolutely thrilled the owners.

ABOVE RIGHT: Built in Duluth for Bayfront Builders, a Parade of Homes project used a great deal of stone. The house was beautiful, but the full-stone bathroom was the show stopper. The crowds seemed to spend a little extra time there, taking in the craftsmanship. Like we predicted, the home sold during its first weekend on the market.

FACING PAGE: When a homeowner in northern Minnesota handed us a photograph of a large-stone fireplace and asked us to build something similar, we were excited about the challenge. Sandstone from a Dunville, Wisconsin, quarry was used; it had been shut down during World War II and had recently reopened, letting us gather the large stones we needed. With some measuring up to 12 feet long, the stones presented a real difficulty as we tried to get them into the house and installed with accuracy. But once again, our dedication and passion for the job paid off, and the result is one of our finest pieces of stonework.

Photographs by Johnston Masonry

MG McGrath Architectural Sheet Metal

Maplewood, Minnesota

"Stainless steel, titanium, zinc, copper—each has a uniquely beautiful aesthetic. No building is complete without a touch of crafted metal."

—Michael McGrath Jr.

ABOVE & FACING PAGE: There are infinite ways to express a concept in architectural sheet metal. In the early '80s our vision was to revolutionize how people think of the art form. I think we've made great progress, having worked with top-tier architects across the country and grown our studio to more than a hundred talented professionals while maintaining an artisan culture. Whether crafting a dramatic sunshade or a paneling system for an entire building, we design with the site in mind. We collaborate with architects and designers to understand each project's needs, develop concepts, determine the most appropriate fabrication and installation techniques, select the right material and finish and, ultimately, create and install the large-scale work of sheet metal art.

Photographs by Greg Anderson

"Metal is a wonderful substance all on its own, but the way it's fabricated, distressed, bent, molded, treated or stained can dramatically alter and enhance its presentation."

—Michael McGrath Jr.

ABOVE: In this age of green design, zinc panels made of a high-recycled content are a great choice. In addition to their inherently eco-friendly composition, they have a long life and can be easily recycled or repurposed later on. We always appreciate the opportunity to perform both glass and metal installation, because that's the best way to fully integrate the systems. Wrapping the metal around the edges of windows requires great planning and precision.

FACING PAGE: Creativity and craftsmanship are our priorities, so it doesn't matter if we're covering several hundred thousand square feet of a building in metal or making a custom fireplace surround—we're going to give it our all. Metal is amazingly versatile. It can be used to make a dramatic impact or gracefully yield to the beauty of nature. Either way, it has staying power.
Photographs by Greg Anderson

"The options for architectural metal can be a bit overwhelming, but it's hard to go wrong."

—Michael McGrath Jr.

ABOVE: Façade, roof, architectural accent, interior design detail or anything else people can come up with—we've made them all happen. The bridge is a fine representation of the textural possibilities of stainless steel. Though metal is characteristically a cold surface, we can make it feel so warm, inviting and sculptural.

FACING PAGE TOP: Traditionally, sheet metal has two dimensions, horizontal and vertical. By creating a third, we gave the design incredible texture and we gave ourselves quite a challenge in terms of forming the panels and getting them to seamlessly connect. Computer modeling programs assist our craftsmen so that projects can be done efficiently.

FACING PAGE BOTTOM: Echoing its mountainous surroundings, the home's roof has more than 60 roughs that jet out at different angles. Now that's a custom metal job. We combined materials and finishes—crystal titanium and patinaed copper—to produce a rich and extremely unique effect.
Photographs by Greg Anderson

"Perfection is acceptable."

—Eric Dudley

ABOVE: Much of the interior stone work we do is on high-end homes in our region. Our style reflects whatever the homeowner wants—without sacrificing an ounce of quality. The end result is the most important aspect of the work; we aren't looking to cut any corners. Because of this, top builders and architects work exclusively with us. For an MS&I Building Company home, we constructed a multiuse buffet, adding clean lines and strength to the room.
Photograph by Joanne Marquette

FACING PAGE: A large home addition and renovation utilized Copper Canyon stone. The pieces are an inch-and-a-quarter thick, laminated to two-and-a-half inches, with bullnose edging. Perimeter tops have full-height backsplash. All of the work is book matched, which means we've virtually eliminated the seams' visibility. In the foreground is a two-tiered island; a second island in the background is equipped with a tapanyaki grill—a specialized feature for both professional chefs and home cooks. Since the kitchen typically serves as the hub of the house, it is important for the room to have a comfortable, easy flow. Guests and homeowners have to feel relaxed in the most-used room—our work ensures that.
Photograph by Greg Page—Page Studios Inc.

"No matter the project, we work as if the pieces were going in our own homes. We invest the necessary resources, whether it be time, money or extra materials."

—Eric Dudley

ABOVE: Calcutta Gold marble vanity with a mitered drop edge makes this bathroom stand out. One-and-a-quarter-inch sidepieces, toe kicks and backsplash between the mirrors and make-up table add luxurious detail to the design.
Photograph by Jeanne Marquette

FACING PAGE: Many elements make the bathroom dramatic. Rope lighting was used to complement the translucent Arco Onyx vanity with a backlit backsplash and a vessel sink. Again, book matching gives the illusion of a single stone piece.
Photograph by Jill Greer

"Realistic expectations are important. Homeowners shouldn't settle for anything less than what they want—but it has to be a realistic vision."

—Eric Dudley

ABOVE LEFT: The undermount sink detail shows the consistent beauty of Jurassic Black granite all the way through the piece. Intriguing and stunning in one fell swoop, the design allows nature and modernity to mix—stone sequences blend beautifully with a stainless steel sink.
Photograph by Jeanne Marquette

ABOVE RIGHT: Overhang details can reveal a great deal about the craftsmanship of a job. For a Juparana Colombo granite island, two three-quarter-inch stone pieces were laminated together to make an inch-and-a-half top. Edge details on each layer create a waterfall effect, flowing with varying radiuses. We emphasized the high quality materials through an attractive design—essentially joining two islands.
Photograph by Jeanne Marquette

FACING PAGE TOP: Granite, called Taupe, was used for the bar top, complemented by Black Galaxy granite for the lower and back bar. Full of personality and fun, the MS&I home bar serves as the perfect spot to entertain visitors.
Photograph by Jill Greer

FACING PAGE BOTTOM: A Forest Lake residence offers its owners a dream kitchen with an ideal layout, flowing and smooth, thanks to Melanie Newville of Newville Designs. Built up two-and-a-half inches, the Juparana Classico Supreme granite is used for the island with raised bar—42-inch elevation—and perimeter countertops. A rotisserie oven and pot filler make the space fit for a chef.
Photograph by Jeanne Marquette

SUNRAY CABINETS

Shakopee, Minnesota

"We have developed relationships of trust and respect with many of the area's top architects and designers. Our clients recognize and appreciate the creative energy that results."

—Scott Terwilliger

ABOVE & FACING PAGE: Our working relationship with some of the region's best architects and contractors is in part due to a mutual understanding of quality, from a simple anigre loft kitchen to a master suite fireplace setting. Collaboration of the design team and an insistence on quality are key to perfect results.

Above photograph by Jill Greer
Facing page photograph courtesy of MS&I

"As a custom shop, we specialize in innovative and unique work that is tailored for a specific client or project. To grasp the design intent we often will meet with clients multiple times in order to fully understand their vision."

—Scott Terwilliger

ABOVE: To provide warmth and luxury, domestic cherry was used throughout a master bath project, giving the homeowner a space that rivals the finest spa.
Photograph courtesy of MS&I

FACING PAGE: The material composition of the kitchen turned out exactly as the client envisioned. The combination of exotic stone counters and stainless steel, Swiss pear and makore cabinets makes the room truly stand out. The open design and highly functional space, such as the corner banquette, bar and multiple workstations, give the kitchen a timelessness that only comes with meticulous planning.
Photographs courtesy of Streeter & Associates

"Every project is like a new book, the uniqueness of each being driven by the client and the selected design team. The end product, not fully realized until completion of the work, typically exceeds all expectations."

—Scott Terwilliger

ABOVE: Quartersawn walnut with inlaid antique porcelain tiles surrounds a flat-screen television, giving a unique blend of classic contemporary style to the room. All the cabinet niches include side-halogen lighting to better accent the client's sculpture collection.

FACING PAGE: Our cabinetry can appear in multiple ways. Curio cabinets were designed and fabricated to mirror the curved gallery walls and to highlight the client's collectables. Side lighting, radius glass shelves and doors dramatically enhance the presentation.
Photographs by Jill Greer

BLASTED ART INC

Minneapolis, Minnesota

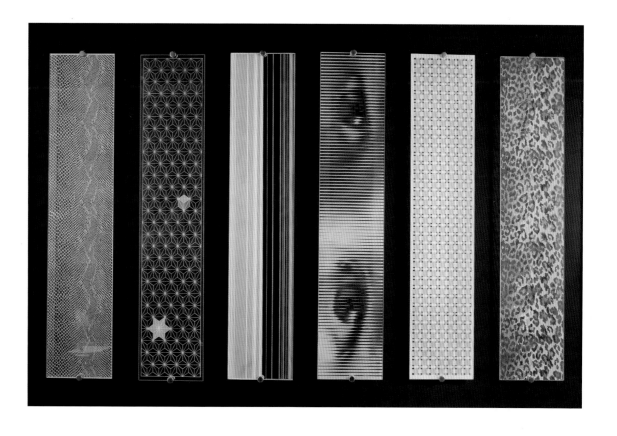

"Hard, cold, yet unmistakably fragile, glass offers a multitude of characteristics. My work brings out its artistic integrity."

—Kerry Dikken

ABOVE: Growing up on a farm, I became enamored with the effects of basic erosion and the results it created. Often, I would watch small pieces of grain slowly wear down the interior of a wooden elevator until patterns appeared. Something so simple yielded beautiful results. Eventually, I began working in design and print production. And then I integrated my hobby of creative sandblasting—a process that has strong similarities to my childhood fascination. Instead of sending the design to a printing press once design production is complete, we sandblast it. The possibilities are unlimited with this technique, and my showroom reveals that. A studio sampling of patterns shows off a method that sandblasts both sides of glass, utilizing the advantages of the medium. Although the process can become painstaking, the results are worth it—the human eye picks up the detailed subtleties of the double-sided pattern.

FACING PAGE: Specifically made for a condominium project, I created a three-quarter-inch-thick vanity top and glass sink for a sleek, streamlined look. The feel is clean and open with absolutely nothing to hide.
Photographs by TK Studios

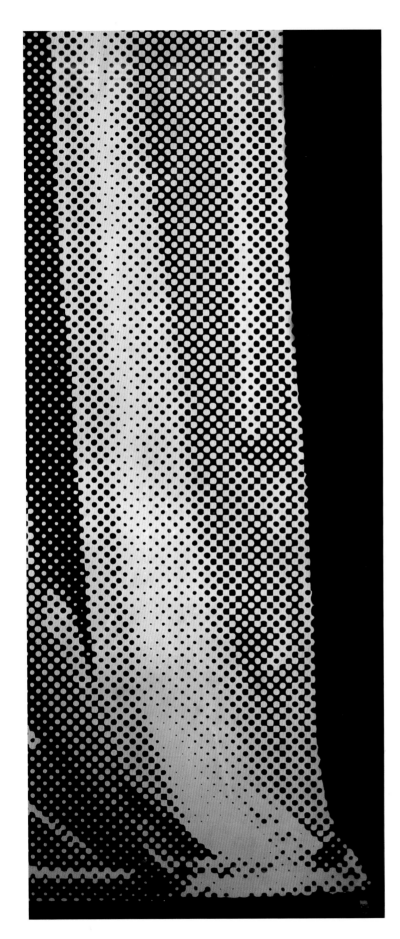

ABOVE & LEFT: When a dot pattern is sandblasted onto glass, the curtain-like effect is remarkable. From afar, the window appears to have streaming, light curtains but an up-close glance shows the meticulous method used to create the piece. The image allures viewers, engaging them in a multidimensional dynamic. When illuminated from the front of the home, the windows become opaque and allow for a bit of privacy. Backlighting or front lighting gives different excitement to the illusion. This same technique is ideal for shower doors and partitions, as well. Eventually, I'd love to create custom moire patterns for an entire office building, offering an air of life, movement and vibrancy to the exterior. The results would be stunning.
Renderings by Chris Hayden

FACING PAGE: A dungeon-dark basement turns into a beautifully lit lower level, functioning as a den or workspace. We installed a glass wall to let light beam through and open up the space. The sandblasting allows this while still offering privacy.
Photographs by Scott Ervin

"We can sandblast anything, from stone to metal to glass to leather or denim—any solid surface."

—Kerry Dikken

CHARLES R. STINSON ARCHITECTS

Deephaven, Minnesota

"It makes sense that a Stinson homeowner would become a commercial client. Why shouldn't a public building have all the details and beauty of a well-planned home?"

—Charles Stinson

ABOVE: When the North American Financial Center wanted to build a banking facility, I knew that the structure would serve as a common gathering place. It had to be light-filled, welcoming and accommodating on every level. The bank's blue-tinted, low-e windows are framed with Douglas fir to enhance the residential feel. I specified Douglas fir for floors, millwork, information desks and teller stations to achieve the warmth I envisioned. Tan and gold ceramic tile complements the limestone and custom limestone concrete block on the walls and fireplace. Heated and cooled by geothermal wells beneath the parking lot, the building also houses a community room, coffee shop and outdoor courtyard, an insurance agency and two separate offices.

FACING PAGE: Efficient and stunning, the 23,000-square-foot structure's strong horizontal planes move from the stucco exterior to an interior atrium with clerestory windows, soffits and a second-floor terrace that serves as an employee lounge. The horizontals join at a 40-foot-tall fireplace in the center of the atrium, anchoring the building and symbolizing the bank's strength, longevity and responsibility as a financial hearth to the community.
Photographs by Peter Bastianelli-Kerze

"Homes are all about the process and the stories that we develop along the way."

—Tom Meyer

elements of design

At MS&R, the design process is intimate and reflective. The team wants clients to see themselves in their finished home. They believe the best homes come from relationships that are mutually respectful, open and insightful.

MS&R's approach to residential design is highly collaborative and often results in life-long friendships between designer and homeowner. The firm believes that the best creative work is a taut marriage of large insights and small details. Experience teaches that clients may buy inspiration, but they live with the details.

Two homes in particular represent two distinct lifestyles: the growing young family and the active retired couple. The common thread between both projects is architect Tom Meyer. Interior design associate Jodi Gillespie collaborated with Tom on the loft while interior design principal Traci Lesneski oversees MS&R's interior architecture practice, which includes residential, corporate and cultural projects. They each share the unique stories and insights they've gained from designing the two homes.

MEYER, SCHERER & ROCKCASTLE, LTD.

"She thought of the process broadly, like a chapter in her life. If someone had just delivered this house to her, it wouldn't have been right."

—Tom Meyer

ABOVE & PREVIOUS PAGES: The homeowner, a former architecture student of Tom's, wanted to blend modern and romantic elements into her young family's Orono home. Sited on 20 acres of rolling prairie overlooking a wetland, the house features a roofline that was inspired by a photo of an old, weathered, bent and twisted barn. The image was one of a collection of clippings and writings collected by the homeowner. On the back of this particular photograph, she wrote "I love the extraordinary layering of time here." The image and note became our inspiration. The gable rafters change slope along the length of the house, forming an S-shaped ridge line that alludes to the sagging barn roof. We carefully aligned the windows to frame views of the surrounding prairie, pond and fruit orchard.
Photographs by Assassi Productions

FACING PAGE: Memories have been built, almost literally, into the house. Several doors and fireplace mantels are from Rome and Umbria, the location of the homeowners' honeymoon. Tom and the homeowner returned to Italy to choose each piece and listen to the stories of the sellers. The New York bluestone used both in the interior and on the exterior was chosen by the homeowner after she made several visits to quarries. Stone contrasts with reclaimed materials. Douglas fir beams once used in a U.S. Air Force hangar and teak floorboards from a former Zimbabwe railroad line are used in the dining room and entryway.
Photographs by Pete Sieger

"We spend more time talking with clients about how they live than we do picking out furnishings or paint color. It's the small insights that have impact."

—Jodi Gillespie

ABOVE LEFT: Upstairs, the hallway undulates beneath the sloping beam roof, linking the master suite with the children's bedrooms. The children run their fingers across the custom-designed railing, creating a series of harp-like notes as their fingers pluck the railing wires. Sounds associated with family were carefully incorporated into the design.
Photograph by Pete Sieger

ABOVE RIGHT: The sitting room in the master suite provides views to the outside while offering intimate privacy inside. Purchased in Rome, the fireplace mantel reminds the homeowners of their honeymoon.
Photograph by Assassi Productions

FACING PAGE LEFT: A relaxed way of life defines the house. Rooms flow into one another in a natural way; and we used wood and stone materials to create warmth.
Photograph by Pete Sieger

FACING PAGE RIGHT: Huge ancient timbers were milled to create beams.
Photograph by Pete Sieger

ABOVE: The industrial heritage of the original Minneapolis building provides the foundation for the design of this riverfront loft. Blending old and new, we retained the loft's open floorplan but defined private areas such as the bath, without losing the industrial feel that attracted the homeowners. Mill-finish steel and frosted glass simultaneously provide privacy and transparency.

FACING PAGE: With views of the Mississippi River, the apartment spans half of the old utility building's ninth floor. Large industrial windows frame dramatic views of the Mississippi River's only waterfall, while flooding the interior space with warm daylight. The idea is to let light flow through the space and give a sense of continuous space. A nod to the wife's career as a dancer, the floor was constructed as a sprung dance floor providing cushioning under foot.
Photographs by George Heinrich

"Contrast and juxtaposition are at play in this space. The warm wood against the exposed ceiling pipes demonstrates how well sophisticated materials and practical features can blend."

—Traci Lesneski

RIGHT: Universal design features such as custom grab bars and wider door openings allow the retired couple to age gracefully in the home. Open kitchen shelves make for easy access since everything is visible and easy to find. Custom four-finger-hole drawers accommodate arthritic hands.

FACING PAGE: The kitchen and dining area can seat as many as 30 people—which is perfect for entertaining. Combined with the loose aesthetic of the interior, the overall transparency gives a relaxed feeling to the entire apartment.
Photographs by George Heinrich

"The most intimate spaces of a home should be warm and welcoming."

—Tom Meyer

LEFT: The interior reuses 75 percent of the clients' existing furniture, accessories and art. A chandelier, custom-made by the client's son, rises and lowers above the dining room table, and tiles, handmade by the couple's daughter-in-law, surround the bathtub and shower. A sculpted work from the wife's mother sits in the foyer.

FACING PAGE: Throughout the space, we designed the lighting plan to be plentiful without creating glare. Closet track lighting is adjustable as are the shelves and rods. Drawer units are raised off the floor for easier access. The master bath retains an open feel, with a vanity set in front of a glass wall that overlooks a small terrace. A large radiator system that circulates hot water sits in front of the windows, warming the bathroom.
Photographs by George Heinrich

"We have moved beyond just cabinets—we design and create. Our team operates as a cohesive group to bring every aspect of the home together."

—Michelle Bloyd

ABOVE: The drama of contrast takes over for a condominium we designed; frosted glass meets stainless steel and noche marble island-top meets dark wood. Stained charcoal grey flooring lies beneath the island, surrounded by a row of glossy cocoa tile that gives the entire piece a floating effect.

FACING PAGE: For a kitchen with transitional style, we used cherry cabinets and a granite called Opalescence. Elements like the door style and black trim make the kitchen so appealing. In an unlikely combination that serves as the center of focus, the stainless steel hood sits over a glass-block partition that peeks into a hallway.
Photographs by Jim Gallop

"Anything can work if it's designed right. Details and creativity can fit into any price range."

—Michelle Bloyd

ABOVE: Quartersawn oak with cocoa staining results in rich, textural woodwork Close attention to detail becomes apparent with a backlit floating mirror, toe-lit tumbled marble on floors and beautifully curved vanity space and shower wall.
Photograph by Jim Gallop

FACING PAGE TOP: The juxtaposed waves and angles take over the master bathroom, giving it comfort and style. Curves of the ceiling and bathtub meet unexpectedly with the angles of the linear cabinetry.
Photograph by LandMark Photography

FACING PAGE BOTTOM: Bathrooms all have personalities of their own. An environmentally conscious powder bath features renewable Lyptus wood cabinets. Metallic sheen coats the tile with tinges of pewter and bronze. Glass vessels and glass tiles sit amongst the Cambria countertop, resulting in an organic yet elegant space.
Photograph by Jim Gallop

"Find a unifying factor, such
as color, shape or feeling,
and use that to create
a balance and cohesion
within your home."

—Michelle Bloyd

RIGHT: Driftwood cabinets with a coffee glaze give way to a coffered ceiling, while walnut appears behind the shelves to coordinate with the floor. Because woodwork is a long-term investment, timelessness becomes critical. The room has a distinct style and yet still maintains that timeless quality, continually rewarding to the homeowners.
Photograph by LandMark Photography

FACING PAGE TOP: Homeowners should be completely thrilled with their new space and at ease in the environment. A kitchen we worked on provided just that to the residents. We stained maple-colored cabinets with driftwood coffee glaze that really let the olive undertones come through. The two-toned room contrasts the clean maple color with the room's strong presence of knotty alder. Above the stove, a hood shows off careful craftsmanship, woven with copper and acid, etched into dark brown.
Photograph by Jim Gallop

FACING PAGE BOTTOM: Up-close details reveal distressed Lyptus moulding and a glass cabinet with a mitered door and carefully selected knobs.
Photographs by Jim Gallop

"Thinking of building or remodeling? Look at magazines, art and model homes to get ideas for architectural planning and décor. But always be open and willing to let the design evolve."

—Michelle Bloyd

RIGHT: A mixture of textures can be the key to a fun room. Different shapes, sizes and surfaces bring spaces to life: a smooth, curving mantel touches the sharp angles of cherry mocha cabinetry while spiral-shaped art and Florida coral keystone grab the eye. Materials on the furniture reveal the same diversity, from traditional paisley to modern geometric prints.
Photograph by LandMark Photography

ENTERTAINMENT DESIGNS, INC.

Minneapolis, Minnesota

"Once people experience a well-designed home entertainment system, they are hard-pressed to set foot in a public venue."

—David Peterson

ABOVE & FACING PAGE: Welcomed by an intricate mahogany door, the Berger theater has everything movie-goers—young and old—would want. The lobby offers a full candy counter and a ticket attendant with a wine room just off to the side. In the span of one year, we built the ultimate home cinema. Working with the homebuilder, Steiner & Koppleman, we constructed the theatre of Spancrete® and located it underneath the turn-around driveway at the front of the house. The lower-level space uses an HVAC system to maintain air circulation and keep the perfect temperature.
Photographs courtesy of Entertainment Designs, Inc.

"A finely appointed home theater can also function as a comfortable living room, whether or not a film is rolling."

—David Peterson

ABOVE & FACING PAGE: In traditional bijou fashion, the theater is adorned with plush, rich textures and colors. A nine-foot-deep performance stage, fiber optic star ceiling and hidden control room add to the classic cinema setting that accommodates small groups or large crowds. No modern amenity is left behind; Cinema Tech chairs, a state-of-the-art sound system, high-definition satellite and a Blu-Ray player offer the ultimate experience.
Photographs courtesy of Entertainment Designs, Inc.

"It's not just about the way a theater looks. Performance is critical."

—David Peterson

RIGHT: Whether we design a family room or a large theater, our goal is the same. We aim for comfort; we want people to spend time in these spaces even when they aren't watching a film. To achieve this level of luxury, no detail is forgotten. We take care of everything, from complete acoustic design and engineering to motorized leather seating systems. Whole-house audio and video distribution, camera surveillance and digital phone systems are also available to homeowners—and we'll travel across the country to design and install it. Projects have spanned the map, from California to Florida with many locations in between.

FACING PAGE: Designed by SKD Architects, the Ostrander home deserved a theater that matched its elegance. Working with the homeowner as the interior designer, we created a modern, calming cinematic space. Cove lighting, accent lighting and sleek sconces help capture the ambience of a 1930s' New York hotel lobby. *Photographs courtesy of Entertainment Designs, Inc.*

ABOVE & FACING PAGE BOTTOM LEFT: With the use of extensive computer planning, we crafted the ultimate audio-visual experience—the Cook theater. Designed before ever building the room, the sound system delivers film dialogue with amazing clarity. Cut to resemble the traditional pattern of an argyle sweater, the walls' panels conceal RPG acoustic tools, which enable the room to maintain complete audio control. The theater's acoustic treatments also provide isolation from the rest of the home, allowing viewers to enjoy the full frequency and full volume range any time of the day or night.

FACING PAGE TOP & BOTTOM RIGHT: Sketched out on four cocktail napkins at the Hazeltine National Golf Club, a friend's living space turned into a retreat. I designed a highly personalized room that he could use as an escape. With the feel of an old-fashioned men's supper club, the room pays homage to the homeowner's favorite golf courses with glowing glass cabinets. The emblems of Tonto Verde, Hazeltine and Bear Path appear in detailed etched glass on either side of the flat-screen. For complete privacy, a sliding bookcase cuts off access to the next room and offers an air of isolation. Rich leather seating and carefully coordinated décor bring the room together—nothing is more relaxing.
Photographs courtesy of Entertainment Designs, Inc.

"I like to build homes that excite. This happens by using something a little differently: a window placement, a different technique done perfectly or a new and unique material that surprises."

—Bud Dropps

ABOVE: Calming, secluded and always welcoming, a log home serves as a retreat for a Twin Cities family. Built to enjoy the natural surroundings, the home is anchored on the shores of north central Minnesota's Big Sandy Lake. We ensured that views of the water were available throughout, whether standing in the second-level owner's suite, one of the two kitchens or the great room. Stone walls, walking paths and an old-fashioned carriage house add to the rustic charm of the retreat property.

FACING PAGE: A double-sided fireplace surrounded with stone emphasizes the warmth and comfort in the home's library while maintaining openness. Knotty alderwood, a coffered ceiling, thoughtful millwork and rich reds offer a depth to the room.
Photographs by Kelly Povo

"My contributions are to create the 'art of space.' A little spunk, a splash of color and a unique twist are always fun to discover in a home."

—Jim Kuiken

ABOVE & FACING PAGE BOTTOM LEFT: A home featured in the country's largest Parade of Homes takes full advantage of the natural landscaped setting. We placed horizontal windows throughout the kitchen and dinette, allowing the owners panoramic views of the outdoors. Nature's role is clear at every glance; American walnut makes up the warm glow of flooring while the cabinetry uses horizontal-grained Douglas fir to achieve its look. Also surrounded with Douglas fir, the fireplace is encased with large Italian porcelain tiles. Montana ledge stone is perfectly stacked on the walls of the universal room where the grand piano sets the tone.

FACING PAGE TOP: A 12-foot center island with bookend cabinets and stormy night granite owns the center of attention in the highly functional and captivating kitchen. While in the great room, the vault floats upon the illuminated recessed soffit, supporting the illusion of having no apparent end or limit. Again, nature's role is evident through the floor-to-ceiling windows.

FACING PAGE BOTTOM RIGHT: Pure craftsmanship is featured in the owner's bath. Illuminated above and below, a floating vanity with canopy has stacked drawers down the center of its design—or so it appears. The center space is actually comprised of a door, carefully blended into the piece for a seamless look. A reflection of the large window cascades natural light into the room at each private sink basin, set on Mesabi honed granite.
Photographs by Kelly Povo

"Interpreting the client's desires is the real art of this business. Tight woodwork, proper mechanicals and superb finishes should be a given."

—Bud Dropps

ABOVE: It's important to bring nature into a home. When we began designing and building a home on a property with a beautiful pond, we knew that amenity had to be included inside the home. Large windows let the residents remember their location, with the views providing a sensation of floating atop the water. The sun's orientation dictates the room's mood; from bright and cheery in the morning light, to mellow and contemplative as the shadows fall.

FACING PAGE: Elements like bamboo flooring and the fireplace's ceramic bowl filled with smooth stones make the space unforgettable. Maple and African mahogany cabinetry plays beautifully off of the polished emerald pearl granite countertops. The area brings modern elegance and function into one space.
Photographs by Kelly Povo

ALDO, INC.

Minnetonka, Minnesota

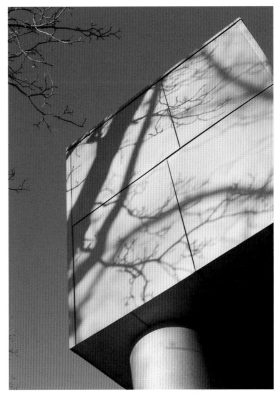

"Our father, Alan Opheim, founded this company on taking pride in doing a job right the first time and putting his signature to it. And that's the underlying principle of our company."

—Kurt Opheim

ABOVE & FACING PAGE: Working with Frank Gehry is a once-in-a-lifetime opportunity, so we jumped at the chance to collaborate with him on a guesthouse in Orono. Our craftsmanship had to be precise. We amended the design to ensure that the sheet metal and roofing could withstand Minnesota winters but didn't compromise Gehry's vision in the slightest. Now donated to the University of St. Thomas, the house features multiple textures, including galvanized and pre-finished black metal for the tower. *Photographs by Mike Ekern, University of St. Thomas*

"Beginning with our parents' foundation, three generations of family work in the firm—our name is on the line with every project."

—Terri Berry

ABOVE & FACING PAGE TOP: Copper gutters, a concave copper roof and charming round windows make an MS&I playhouse absolutely enchanting. Built for an auction at a Ferndale residence, the elaborate playhouse raised money for Common Bond Communities, a non-profit developer of affordable homes.

FACING PAGE BOTTOM: We constructed innovative ways of catching the rain for an MS&I and SKD home. Detailing on the copper eaves reveals the use of rain chains—both effective and stunning.
Photographs by Jill Greer, courtesy of SKD Architects and MS&I Building Company

"Our father has an artist's soul. And all of our work shows a bit of that. His drive to perpetually create has infused our projects with an imaginative spirit."

—Steve Opheim

ABOVE & FACING PAGE: Traveling around the world has offered our projects a new perspective. We've been across the Midwest, California, Arizona and as far as Korea, giving our at-home work an edge. For a Madeline Island sailing cabin on Lake Superior, we crafted standing seam roofs and gutters made of brilliant copper that make the house stand out. And simple soffit details for a Delano home add symmetrical style.
Above photograph by Dan Mulrennan, courtesy of SKD Architects
Facing page top photograph by Dan Mulrennan, courtesy of SKD Architects
Facing page bottom photograph by Ashley Berg

"Classically, trompe l'oeil techniques required an extreme understanding of perspective and realism. Today's standards are no different. Artists using this method should have their arms wrapped firmly around artistic tradition and burgeoning trends. It's not about playing it safe; it's about creating art."

—Carter Averbeck

ABOVE LEFT: Harking back to the Art Deco days of New York, we used an authentic Venetian plaster with a highly burnished sheen to create a polished marble surface in a foyer to reflect the style of an era gone by. Carved out sections were then carefully filled with silver leaf to reveal a fantasy-like starburst.

ABOVE RIGHT: Like the alluring interior of a pearl, a matte metallic finish shimmers and catches the eye in the opalescent gem of a powder room.

FACING PAGE: Honoring the works of Russian-born Mark Rothko, our color technique gives credit to his pioneering style. We used his patterning of color but with a Venetian plaster fade instead of the traditional application—innovation never disappoints. Instead of a single hue, the wall begins with a deep chocolate brown and dissipates to a shade of golden green apple.
Photographs by Greg Page, Page Photography

"I have a theater background, which is reflected in my work. There is a vivid and sometimes delicate element of life that appears throughout."

—Carter Averbeck

ABOVE: When I began planning a monochromatic master bedroom mural, I immediately knew that my experience with architectural history would come in handy. Tutored by a fresco master during my studies, I prefer natural ingredients to synthetic. Animal fat combined with crushed pigments gave color to the room's cracked linen fresco in a showcase home. The distinct feel of a French Normandy interior is present, including the suggestion of a Romanticist's forgotten mural.

FACING PAGE: My work reaches across a broad range of topics. Some depictions reveal mythological tales while others give hints into real life. A peek at the wall in the master bedroom shows a scene of Midas with his unfortunate donkey ears, looking onto a dancing circle of female debauchery. A dome ceiling mural however, reveals the portraits of a couple's children, playing violins and trumpets while watching over the home.

Photographs by Greg Page, Page Photography

"If green principles are important to homeowners, there is no reason they cannot find a painter who agrees. Artists trained in the classical sense have an advantage in knowing how to use sustainable products like eggs, clay, animal fat and even beer, in place of harsh chemical counterparts."

—Carter Averbeck

RIGHT: These walls mimic the earthy beauty of an old tree trunk with an application of a specialized plaster called Sabbia. Granular and brushed with marble dust afterward, the design gets people's attention.

FACING PAGE: Regardless of the space, creativity and innovation can take over. What's life without rocking the boat a little? Luminescent walls came from the application of gold leaf finishes to a home's interior. By throwing acid on it and letting a rainbow of colors emerge, the unpredictable becomes a distinct patina. Water halts the acid's progress; then we layer silver and copper leaf to let all three metal finishes show. A lobby area required a little more reserve with that same luster; here we used a shimmering Venetian plaster fade as a backdrop to simple, yet contemporary décor. A bronze dome caps off the elegant appearance.
Photographs by Greg Page, Page Photography

WILLIE WILLETTE WORKS

Minneapolis, Minnesota

"When people see my work, I don't want them to ask what store it came from. Every piece I create is one of a kind—and I want that to be evident."

—Willie Willette

ABOVE & FACING PAGE: To diminish the excess space in a couple's home, we built a solid walnut bookcase that was both simple and ingenious. It works with the air ducts and remains in sync with the design of the room— straightforward without pretension. Even the detailing stays with the furniture's bare-bones appeal, using recovered piano keys as pins.
Photographs by Paul Nelson Photography

"You want a rocket ship? We can build it."
—Willie Willette

ABOVE: The African Bubinga table demonstrates our appreciation for non-studio, non-manufactured work. After meeting up with a Minnesota farmer who collects live edge planks, I saw the possibility for a memorable, organic table. Maintaining the integrity of the entire slab was a top priority, which is why a minimal, Eastern-inspired design works. Surrounding antique chairs serve to emphasize, not overpower, the aesthetic merit of the live edge wood.

FACING PAGE: It took five prototypes and nearly two months to perfect the Melissa chair, well worth the effort and wait. Fully handmade and locally sourced, the chair has become an all-around favorite. As the models progressed, the design became streamlined, lightened in mass and softened in curve. The original photographs depicted Western, rustic seating that turned into the most comfortable contemporary furniture once we finished. Solid walnut make-up meets modern scallops and simple geometry, placing it in the most appealing gap between traditional and modern. If we hadn't pushed the client, the piece never would have come about. That's why we focus on strong collaboration, exchanging ideas and evolving. Every mind can open.
Photographs by Paul Nelson Photography

"Not everything is a Baroque masterpiece; and we don't want it to be. We make pieces that have use. Function is key. Without function, you have failure."

—Willie Willette

ABOVE: When the owners of a high-end Italian furniture store needed a front desk for their shop, they wanted something that wouldn't detract from their pieces. So we came up with a flash-free, black desk to greet shoppers at the door. Cantilevered four feet and bolted to the floor, the monolith slab is undoubtedly an original.

FACING PAGE: We love working with creative clients; ideas beget ideas. At first, I resisted the thought of silver on a project made of rich walnut: twin bookcases and consoles. But the homeowner insisted and I listened. It's very possible to be uncompromising on quality yet completely open to new ideas.
Photographs by Paul Nelson Photography

HOLLOW ROCK DESIGNS

"With a few tons of concrete and a reliable pick-up truck, we can make anything work."

—Patricia Bigelow

ABOVE & FACING PAGE: Our concrete designs are different. And after taking our sinks to a Kitchen and Bath Association tradeshow, we realized just how true this is. Pushing us into the industry and letting us really stand out as artisans among the crowd, trade shows have given us the opportunity to travel all over the country and show off our work. The designs are as distinct as the people who buy them. For a young Minnesota bachelor who lives in the city, we built a one-ton loft installation that had a stainless steel trough attached, exposing the concrete as the back wall. After blocking off the streets and rolling up our sleeves, we hoisted the project into the apartment with a crane. No obstacle is too big. The design fit him to a "t"—fun with an industrial look and a polished top for mixing drinks.
Photographs courtesy of Crystal Kitchen and Cabinetry

"We've been artists our whole lives. We have the privilege of doing what we love and loving what we do."

—Daniel Bigelow

TOP RIGHT: The sink that turned 10,000 heads—the double farm sink in a Saw Hill-designed kitchen. Appearing in a national magazine, our massive apron sink with a speakeasy look got the country's attention and flooded the telephone lines with questions and requests. No doubt, it was a hit. To achieve the aged appearance that received so much attention, we used patina stains with oxidized copper. The plump, red tomatoes make it look even more appealing. A blacksmith crafted the pot hanger and front plate; the sink edge was made to match the teakwood countertop edges.
Photograph courtesy of Plato Cabinetry and Saw Hill Designs

BOTTOM RIGHT: The initial drawings for a spa bathroom included an all-concrete design: floors, tiles, sinks and countertops. But the final space focused on two vessel sinks from the Pompeii Series, called the Roma. A massive space doesn't have to lose an attention to detail, and this bathroom is the perfect example. Although the room extends far out, two rustic sinks with rich, organic hues draw everyone in.
Photograph courtesy of Ulrich Designs

FACING PAGE: We work with discerning interior designers and architects, so we aim for perfection with every location. Stimmel Design Consultants asked us for sea foam-colored countertops to match a high-end kitchen; and we delivered. A heightened demand for accuracy and precision is always a fun challenge—and we're known for it.
Photographs courtesy of Stimmel Design Group

"The interiors of my living space reflect my life, most prominently the last 35 years of travel and work with the Peace Corps, United Nations, the World Bank and finally, my company Odegard."

—Stephanie Odegard

ABOVE: Two of my hand-knotted silk and wool carpets in the same 17th-century Spanish damask design "Niagara" shown in aceituna—left—and steel grey—right. Since founding my company in 1987, I have produced and imported collections of my own uniquely designed carpets often said to have revolutionized the market. By combining time-revered techniques with contemporary European aesthetics and the highest quality standards, my focus has been on transforming traditional textile art forms and artisanal crafts of developing countries into commercially viable industries capable of raising standards of living for thousands of people. *Photographs by John Bigelow Taylor*

FACING PAGE: Culture, design and beautiful natural materials inform the dining space, revealing influences from India, Tibet, Brazil, Japan, Colombia and Scandinavia. Starting with the carpet, my early Indigo Metok design in silk and wool tweed with raised flowers, shown in tartufo bianco, anchors a Saarinen table surrounded by Wegman chairs draped with hand-woven and embellished Colombian textiles. On top of the table are candleholders from Brazil and above it, an antique wrought iron lamp. One wall is draped by a 20th-century double ikat sari I found in India, and on another, a circa-13th-century Tibetan cut velvet featuring archaic dragons. *Photograph by Antoine Bootz*

"The mission of Odegard is to marry the interests of the upscale designer market with the age-old tradition of hand knotted carpet weaving, while remaining committed to promoting respect for cultural expression and the environment. I want people to feel good about adding these aesthetic elements to their homes."

—Stephanie Odegard

 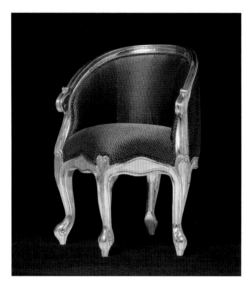 

ABOVE LEFT: My Saba design is a hand-knotted all-wool vegetal dyed carpet. Known for the subtleties created by using all natural materials, worked by hand, the carpet uses the ancient Senna loop knotting technique, which followed the Silk Road from Egypt to Tibet and was later brought to Nepal by the refugees exiled from Tibet—now part of China—in the 1960s. Using a timeless design aesthetic, with a focus on the integrity of the raw materials and weavers' techniques, the Nepalese industry was transformed by the introduction of a new style of modern, clean and minimal hand-knotted Tibetan carpet.

ABOVE MIDDLE: The Raj chair from the Stephanie Odegard Collection is hand carved and clad in pure silver sheeting. This 19th-century Indian chair design is upholstered with hand-woven silk from Laos, from the exquisite textile collection Soie de Lune by Anouphamethong Thammavong, whose design is chosen from his grandmother's personal textile collection. After establishing my hand knotted modern carpet collection and the Odegard name, I expanded the Stephanie Odegard Collection to include "jewelry for the home," objects in marble; silver, copper, bronze and brass-clad, handmade wooden furniture; inlaid surfaces with mother of pearl, semiprecious stones and metals; reverse painted mirror glass; decorative wall surfaces; and hand woven, embroidered and embellished textiles. Most of the work is commissioned through our showrooms and as everything is made by hand, our possibilities are endless.

ABOVE RIGHT: Using a high-low technique in the hand woven construction, Recoleta, shown in ivory, derives its pattern from a sidewalk in Argentina. My carpet production in Nepal involves various techniques, all by hand-shearing sheep, carding wool, hand spinning, dyeing and knotting followed by sophisticated European finishing processes. I am a founding member and on the board of directors of the RugMark Foundation. RugMark independently certifies that each Odegard carpet has been manufactured without the use of child labor.
Photographs by John Bigelow Taylor

FACING PAGE LEFT: Designed by Paul Mathieu exclusively for the Stephanie Odegard Collection, two hand-sculpted marble candelabras and a goblet sit on top of a filigree hand-carved marble table. The bronze lotus candleholders were hand cast by artisans in India. Behind this hangs Odegard's Jetty design, an all-wool hand-knotted carpet, designed in the early '90s.
Photograph by Simon Hare

FACING PAGE RIGHT: The Semainier, copper clad over hand-carved teakwood, is a seven-drawer highboy designed by Paul Mathieu for the Stephanie Odegard Collection and has a drawer for every day of the week.
Photograph by David Paler

SPIZZI MOSAICS

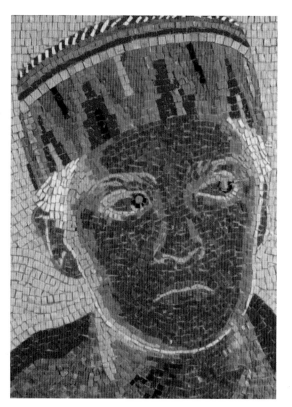

"Rethinking spaces within a home can help integrate art into life. For instance, a backsplash can be so much more than just a functional area. Mosaics bring rooms to life."

—Connie Cohen

ABOVE: I use a specific type of glass tile called smalti, which is imported from Mexico and Italy, to create my mosaics. I cut the glass using a hammer and hardie, a chiseled edge blade used with the hammer—the same tools used in ancient times. Two pieces, created for a private collection, were inspired by personal influences. With Andy Warhol in mind, I turned a personal photograph into an immortalizing image. Striking and intimate, the work reveals a road of exploration I took when designing the piece. Likewise, a self-portrait entitled *Dancing in the Garden*, symbolizes a life journey, which for me is best reflected in art.

FACING PAGE: It seemed appropriate for a self-sustaining cabin in northern Minnesota to take advantage of nature's design. The mosaic tabletop is divided into quarters, representing the four seasons, and displays organic patterns of leaves and outdoor hues.
Photographs by Natalie Domka

ABOVE: When a homeowner commissioned me to create a fireplace surround, I drew from her personality to intuitively gauge what would fit her home. Vibrant, fun and full of life, poppies seemed to be a perfect solution for the mosaic—confirmed by the instant smile that comes to the owner's face each time she passes the fireplace.
Photograph by 20/20 Virtual Tours

FACING PAGE TOP LEFT: Tribulations can inspire art. An amazing woman who asked me to design a piece for her kitchen was celebrating her second year of breast cancer recovery. To honor that journey, I made an abstract expression of the ability to choose a positive path when faced with the unknown.
Photograph by Connie Cohen

FACING PAGE BOTTOM LEFT: Mosaics are not simply craft-like projects completed in a weekend. They are an art form dating back to ancient Greece, marking a visual history of events and cultural lifestyles. When I went to Venice, I had the pleasure of absorbing some of the art's rich history. Browns, greens, golds and silver tones make up this piece, influenced by that trip. Like all of my work, it represents a bigger concept and is woven with my personal experiences.
Photograph by Natalie Domka

FACING PAGE RIGHT: Partly inspired by the Jewish holiday of Tu'Bishvat, one of my works embraced the celebration of trees and the feast of the season's first fruits. Pomegranates ripen before any other crop, making them the first fruit for everyone to enjoy. Because of this, pomegranates signify the promise and hope of a plentiful season. In a vertical mosaic, I symbolized the pomegranate in the bottom center, showing the fruit's intense color while embodying the notion of great possibilities. Running through the pomegranate is the idea of "kundalini"—the awakening of the creative spirit. This piece represents a spiritual shift that has been put into a visual form. As a whole, it reveals a very personal moment in time.
Photograph by Natalie Domka

"Piece by piece, I draw from a world of ideas."
—Connie Cohen

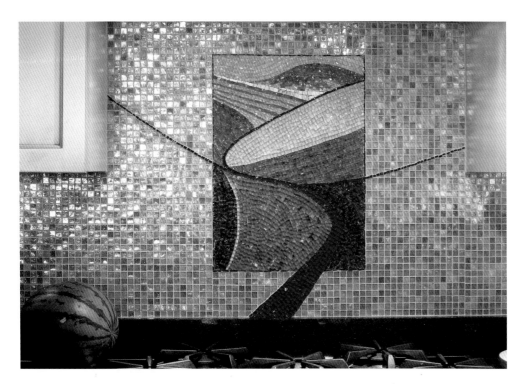

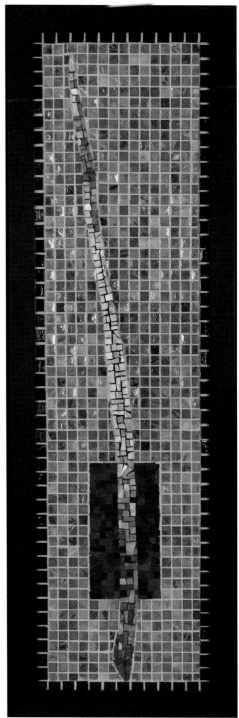

"Elegant, cool, elaborate—our projects have no shortage of excitement."

—Kevin Keenan

living the elements

chapter five

Characterized by its sophisticated projects and approachable manner, Keenan & Sveiven brings common sense and comprehensive beauty to outdoor spaces. Founded in 1990, the firm began with partners Kevin Keenan and Tim Sveiven. While Kevin's background focuses on the design aspect of the process, Tim brings strong field knowledge to the table. But what do they both have in common? They possess a vision: to create landscapes with intricacy and precision. And that vision has been realized, with projects stretching from the Twin Cities, across Minnesota, and into Wisconsin and South Dakota. Their staff includes a range of experts; four landscape architects and approximately six construction crews work on a variety of projects and carry out the designs. Highly personalized and built to last, the homes have earned Keenan & Sveiven a reputation for creating masterpieces.

KEENAN & SVEIVEN

"One look at our work and it's obvious that we love what we do."

—Tim Sveiven

ABOVE & FACING PAGE: Designed by Jason Aune, the landscape architecture for a Midwestern home offers the residents an all-granite patio for lounging or entertaining. Set on pedestals to accommodate subsurface drainage, the highly engineered outdoor space is an extension of a home created by SALA Architects. Natural creeks run through this site, as well as groundwater moving steadily just four or five feet below the surface—a fact that kept our team on its toes. We meticulously plan for every possibility and work around the challenges. Poured concrete columns and cast candleholders surround a bluestone fireplace, while the flagstone patterned inlay gives the feel of an area rug. Dry-stacked walls meander around the pool and provide partitioned structure to create room-like spaces, leading to a secluded studio sitting on the back of the property. A pergola, which doubles as a fence, exhibits function and form. With strong horizontal banding for aesthetic effect, the design shows its practical side by using transparent wire-mesh panels to keep out deer and other wildlife.

PREVIOUS PAGES: Set on a large parcel of land, the outdoor living spaces of this home took two years to design and build. A campus-retreat feel defines the area. The buildings include a main house, a guesthouse on the bluff, two studios, a detached garage, a pool equipment and mechanical building and the poolhouse.
Photographs by Chabrielle

"We take our cues from the architect and from the home. Our design should fit in seamlessly."

—Kevin Keenan

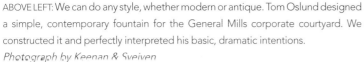

ABOVE LEFT: We can do any style, whether modern or antique. Tom Oslund designed a simple, contemporary fountain for the General Mills corporate courtyard. We constructed it and perfectly interpreted his basic, dramatic intentions.
Photograph by Keenan & Sveiven

ABOVE RIGHT: An elaborate, cottage-like window shows off the feeling of an Old World environment; the design captured a sentiment that gives the home an always-been-there quality.
Photograph by Gallop Studios

FACING PAGE TOP: Todd Irvine worked as the landscape architect on a formal estate home on Lake Minnetonka. The design features a dramatic courtyard and fountain, following the home's style. In addition to lake access, a tennis court sits on the property for private recreation.
Photograph by Greg Ryan and Sally Beyer

FACING PAGE BOTTOM: We designed an Old World European setting for a home that nods to the 19th century. Staying true to the time period, the garden area features a knee-high wrought-iron fence and lush ivy that climbs up the exterior of the master suite and front entrance.
Photograph by Gallop Studios

"We work with a wide array of craftsmen; one of our strengths is the ability to pull everyone together."

—Tim Sveiven

RIGHT: With Todd Irvine as the landscape architect, Streeter & Associates as the homebuilder and Charles Stinson as the architect, the outdoor setting was sure to be a success. Lake Minnetonka sits behind the space, which features lush gardens, a colored concrete pool deck and careful stonework on wide, freestanding columns. Contemporary and sleek, this space makes the outdoors irresistible.
Photograph by Stuart Lorenz

"Challenges are always welcome."
—Kevin Keenan

ABOVE LEFT: Designed by John Johnson, the patio for a TEA2 home shows an intimate setting, giving the family a private, outdoor dining option.
Photograph by Keenan & Sveiven

ABOVE RIGHT: Vibrant vegetation can add a great deal to a home's exterior. John Johnson used it for texture in a front entryway in his design, and Todd Irvine highlighted the wood detailing of a pergola with upward-flourishing vines.
Photographs by Keenan & Sveiven

FACING PAGE: Nightfall brings completely different moods to outdoor living spaces, giving them complex personalities and allowing the residents to create a variety of environments. Jason Aune and SALA Architects capture this idea with strategic illumination. A fireplace and niche candles bring a patio to life, while a Wisconsin summer home is meant to tuck into the woods with a glow of warmth.
Photographs by Chabrielle

"The most rewarding aspect of our work is that we are invited to design and build very personalized outdoor spaces."

—Kevin Keenan

TOP LEFT: Stone dominates an outdoor kitchen designed by John Johnson, complete with a granite bar, arched range hood and tuck-under refrigerator. The stone terrace and fully tiled pool make the space stand out.
Photograph by Jerry Swanson

BOTTOM LEFT: Why even go inside? When we designed a landscape to match a friend's contemporary home, I knew how much time he would spend there. Our designs fit the personalities of the people who occupy them. Stone walls, an outdoor kitchen, a fire pit and an acid-stained concrete pool deck make it the favorite spot to hang out.
Photograph by Joe Miehl

FACING PAGE: Tom Oslund served as the landscape architect for a beautifully executed project, sandwiched comfortably between a simple post-and-beam pergola and white-bricked garden walls. To achieve a sleek, fresh look, the pool's water fills to the brim, creating a smooth plane. The all-granite deck and strong triangular diving stand dramatically add to the polished appearance.
Photograph by Jerry Swanson

"We design, install and maintain colorful, classic gardens and containers that are created to change with the season. A gardener's duties go well beyond merely planting."

—Ann Rieff

ABOVE: Our zone-four growing season is limited, making our gardeners' passion and talent all the more critical to creating lush, vivid gardens. Color is the most important element in creating beautiful compositions. A diverse palette flanks the driveway and adorns the carriage house in the background of a summer garden. Petunias' plum carpet lines the rich beds and peegee Hydrangeas bloom in the background. Karl Foerster grass, Russian sage and Phlox David make up the perennials. Annuals include Cosmos, daisies, Rudbeckia and blue Salvia.
Photograph by Jerry Swanson

FACING PAGE: The plush, densely planted perennial surroundings of an Eden Prairie backyard come to life in early summer. Siberian Iris, Rudbeckia goldsturm and Salvia May Night have a strong presence in the pool's atmosphere, as well as Haddonstone containers filled with red Dipladenias.
Photograph by Stuart Lorenz

"Spring: a sure sign that the long winter is ending and colors will return. Garden bulbs installed during autumn months make their grand entrance in April and May, which is why planning ahead is critical for a successful garden. The transition from spring to summer comes very quickly, ushering in Minnesota's warm days."

—Ann Rieff

TOP RIGHT: A peaceful perennial shade garden is bordered with Hosta whirlwind and salmon Impatiens and filled with Hostas—sieboldiana elegans, sum and substance and sun power—Astilbe Rheinland, Monarda Jacob Kline and variegated Solomon's Seal. We often use borders of annuals or perennials on our garden beds. They provide a feeling of enclosure.

BOTTOM RIGHT: Summer tier gardens accentuate hillside splendor with stone terraces and abundant flowers that smooth a steep slope. Perennials include Coreopsis moon beam, Liatris kobold, Rudbeckia goldsturm and Sedum dragon's blood groundcover; annuals show off the brilliance of Ageratum, Canna city of Portland, white Cosmos, purple fountain grass, sweet potato vine and purple Zinnias.

FACING PAGE TOP: Haddonstone containers nestled against a patio show spring color on the shores of Lake Minnetonka: Narcissus Dutch master, tulip passionale, purple Hyacinth and dynamite yellow pansies. As the seasons change, so do the flowers; the containers continually reflect the time of year.
Photographs by Greg Ryan and Sally Beyer

FACING PAGE BOTTOM: Changed out every season, Gladding Mcbean and Gardenstone containers feature Narcissus ice follies, white Hyacinths and blue pansies in the spring.
Photograph by Ann Rieff

"As the temperatures cool down and the colors of autumn emerge, the clean look of fall containers takes center stage. Mums, kale, asters and grasses change the scene. Splashes of orange from the pumpkins and bittersweet create a Minnesota harvest feeling."

—Ann Rieff

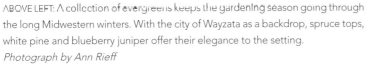

ABOVE LEFT: A collection of evergreens keeps the gardening season going through the long Midwestern winters. With the city of Wayzata as a backdrop, spruce tops, white pine and blueberry juniper offer their elegance to the setting.
Photograph by Ann Rieff

ABOVE RIGHT: As the snow collects on the greens it gives an enchanting look to containers and window boxes. Wintergreens embellished with rose hips, white pine, golden arborvitae, incense cedar and pinecones add beauty and color to an otherwise white and gray season.
Photograph by Ann Rieff

FACING PAGE LEFT: Fall containers amassed with plant material create a welcome entrance. Burgundy, lavender and mauve mums, purple Aster, kale, curly willow stems and standard Eugenias thrive in the cool weather.
Photograph by Greg Ryan and Sally Beyer

FACING PAGE TOP RIGHT: Autumn hues on Mount Curve in Minneapolis include a vibrant range of bronze and orange mums, purple Aster, kale, bittersweet and birch stems.
Photograph by Ann Rieff

FACING PAGE BOTTOM RIGHT: Planted in classic black Gardenstone, yellow and raspberry mums, purple Asters, kale and bittersweet welcome fall's splendor.
Photograph by Ann Rieff

AQUA EDEN

Faribault, Minnesota

"In a fast-pace, high-stress world, people need a chance to slow down, relax and appreciate nature. Our work provides that chance."

—Jake Langeslag

ABOVE: Full-service options include pond, fountain and waterfall construction, as well as waterscape supply and maintenance. The trick is finding exactly what fits each person's needs. For a private residence, a six-foot-wide waterfall curtain matched the vision of the homeowner; the water pours over lush lichens and moss to help establish a backyard sanctuary.

FACING PAGE: What makes for a picturesque setting? Water. When a photo studio contacted us to create the perfect backdrop, I gave them something that would work for multiple angles and sustain a large amount of people. Surrounding forest, peaceful waters and perfectly placed driftwood makes for ideal photographs.

Photographs by Caleb Langeslag, Aqua Eden

"Our goal is to keep people guessing if our water features were actually manmade or placed there by Mother Nature herself. As an outdoor enthusiast and student of ecology, biology and chemistry, I love the challenge of re-creating some of Earth's greatest elements."

—Jake Langeslag

ABOVE: A family that entertains regularly needs outdoor space for their lifestyle; well-planned ponds can provide just the setting for parties and gatherings. The home's large windows let in the view of both the waterscape and the surrounding woodland.

FACING PAGE: One of my first hobbies was bird watching; and when I realized birds possess a strong attraction to moving water, I became enamored with the relationship between the two. Knowing this, I create ponds and waterscapes to complement the natural appeal of animals. The colors of an eastern bluebird become even more vivid and dynamic when set against an organic background. Likewise, the clear waters of a koi pond show off the grace and agility of the ancient Japanese fish below, topped off by a hearty, pink water lily.
Photographs by Caleb Langeslag, Aqua Eden

"A culmination of my education and talents has led to my title as the pondologist™. This role encompasses my commitment to educate the public and further ecological understanding."

—Jake Langeslag

ABOVE: Waterscapes change with the seasons; autumn gives off some of the year's best colors.
Photograph by Jake Langeslag, the pondologist™

FACING PAGE TOP: As each person has different taste, each pond reflects that and takes on a different personality. People often ask us to include statues and decorations, such as a replica of a young fisherman, and others request a purely natural look.
Photograph by Caleb Langeslag, Aqua Eden

FACING PAGE BOTTOM: Once an onlooker notices the details of a waterscape, the charm takes over—the settings draw people in. Whether it's an American robin, vertical rock columns or an overlaid branch, small elements make all the difference.
Facing page bottom left photograph by Jake Langeslag, the pondologist™
Facing page bottom middle & right photographs by Caleb Langeslag, Aqua Eden

BULACH CUSTOM ROCK

Inver Grove Heights, Minnesota

"The results don't just have to look great; each project must be well built and technically correct. Our work is the perfect blend of art and architecture."

—Steve Bulach

ABOVE: A seamless slate texture pattern makes up both the driveway and entry area for this Minnesota home; a stamped circular inset offers contrast and provides a distinct quality to the design.

FACING PAGE: For a large residence with an expansive front area, several terraces were used to help reduce the scale and create a strong sense of entry while maintaining warmth. These levels are connected by a series of steps with cantilevered risers. As vehicles arrive, a central circular water feature accents the square-stamp pattern, laid at 45-degree angles to help further reduce its scale. Landscaping and site furnishings like benches and urns help provide an attractive look to the outdoor setting as a whole.
Photographs by Mark Madsen

"The fact that we've been successful since 1964 proves our ability to fulfill clients' visions. Since the beginning, our design-based, full-service firm has shown its ability to create outstanding work."

—Bob Wallace

ABOVE LEFT: A variety of natural materials comes into one design: stone, wood and brick. Tying them all together is a very spacious two-tiered concrete terrace and pool deck, utilizing a seamless slate textured finish with light-colored concrete coping that complements the cast-in-place wall caps and columns.
Photograph by Bob Wallace

ABOVE RIGHT: Two opposing forces are present: passive and active. Remarkably manmade, the water feature and surrounding rock coping is made from glass fiber reinforced concrete—or GFRC. It makes up the majority of the passive, rock-like surroundings and is complemented by the calm lush green spaces that help provide a naturalistic setting. A large, swim-under shelf lies beneath an energetic waterfall, contributing to a lively feeling in the pool. The stamped and colored concrete pool deck provides access to the pool area from several levels of the home and is available for those more lively pool activities.
Photograph by Bob Wallace

FACING PAGE: Our work comes across as a natural and integral part of the developed site. With ease and confidence, a concrete driveway blends in with a walkway to the home, unified by a strong border. We fit lawnsteps comfortably into the slope of the hill and blended them with the natural stone used to retain the earth, as if Mother Nature had intended it.
Photographs by Emily Anderson

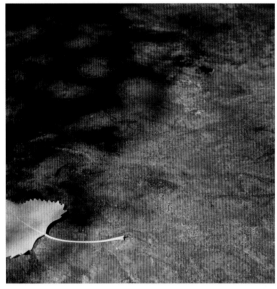

RIGHT: A focus on color, texture and pattern shows up in our work, revealing the broad range of technique and skill that our craftsmen possess. A detailed, hand-painted vineyard theme exhibits rich hues while a warm, vibrant surface grabs the eye; more traditional patterns and shapes give a classic look to indoor and outdoor settings.
Photographs by Emily Anderson and Claire Stokes

FACING PAGE TOP: The rooftop of a luxury apartment complex provides an area of entertainment for the residents. An oversized chess set adds to the fun; the recreation section offers a small practice putting area, sunken spa and barbecue grills. The chess board required careful, technical work. First, we poured a light colored concrete for the entire area. Then we saw cut into the small grids and darkened the appropriate squares with a color wash, followed by a seal to finish.
Photograph by Bob Wallace

FACING PAGE BOTTOM: During an extensive exterior renovation project, the original stone overlay was carefully removed and replaced with colored and textured concrete. The project shows our capacity to innovate, problem solve and work within very specific parameters.
Photograph by Bob Wallace

EARTHSCAPE STONE MASONRY & LANDSCAPE DESIGN

Minnetrista, Minnesota

"It is our sole duty as landscape architects to transcend all boundaries of age, taste, time and place."

—Shane Schaaf

ABOVE: Composed of nearly all reclaimed materials laid in Old World fashion, interjections of dry-stacked stone patty cakes enhance the mischievous flow of visual symmetry. We set limestone slabs vertical to break up the scale of the courtyard wall, then uplit the void to create interest.

FACING PAGE: Our artistic ability is what really makes us stand out; and it's why people come to us. When a homeowner wanted us to create an outdoor design on an elevated terrace, we didn't hold back. A tropical backyard with a large fireplace, waterfall and three fire pits demanded something completely unique—and that's exactly what we built. Pennsylvania bluestone, Utah quartz and Montana and North Dakota moss rock make up the fire pit pattern.
Photographs by Shawn Michienzi

"Our job is fun—and we take fun very seriously."

—Jamie Brown

ABOVE: We're hired for our detailed originality; and we'll be as creative as our clients allow. Sitting alongside a busy roadway, the stone retaining wall had originally been envisioned with a relatively basic design—but basic is boring. So I added a picture-frame pattern to keep it interesting and give onlookers something to think about. But one bump caused the corner to fall and resulted in a mosaic-like, puzzle appearance that we've appropriately titled, Out of the Box. The homeowners love the modern, quirky mix that the design adds to their classic Victorian cedar-shake home.

RIGHT: On-our-toes engineering made a three-dimensional bridge and water flow design really work. A lack of elevation drop made for a more winding, innovative plan that resulted in a strong aesthetic. Organic, ripple-covered rocks fill the bed and give the look of natural erosion, as if the water was actually flowing through the stones.

FACING PAGE TOP: Crossing over the floating limestone bridge, water magically flows between the diamond pattern, eluding the bridge surface, reaching its final destination, the fire room. It's the perfect spot for kids' imaginations to run wild.

FACING PAGE BOTTOM: As visitors are drawn to the rear garden entry, they have to stop, adjust their eyes and wonder if there truly is only one side to the approaching stone arch. Maybe the backlit quartz crystal emerging from the arch grants the courage to pass safely. Make no mistake about it, fossilized nautilus shells and amethyst-blossomed steel flowers crown the entry gate beneath the stone arches' grandeur.

Photographs by Shawn Michienzi

"There always exists the temptation for the author of the design to 'step back' from the installation process. We do not stray from this golden opportunity. And there lies our secret."

—Shane Schaaf

ABOVE & FACING PAGE: Determined to capture the personality of the client, we incorporated downlit amethyst geodes and reclaimed historic hand-carved stone and worked diligently to create a garden space lush with imagination and whimsy. Though grounded by the front courtyard design, one finds no disappointment on the way to the rear garden.
Photographs by Shawn Michienzi

CREPEAU DOCKS

Maple Plain, Minnesota

"Ed Crepeau didn't just revolutionize the docks of Midwestern lakes; he turned them into a regional icon."

—Rick Niccum

ABOVE: Started in 1948, Crepeau Docks introduced a product that changed the industry. Ed Crepeau designed a dock that didn't require the installer to get wet—an unheard of feature at the time. His new steel docks could be adjusted to different water levels and were free of wooden elements that would deteriorate over time. This same simple engineering appears in all of our work today; we constructed this dock with maintenance-free Titan decking and all aluminum components on Lake Minnetonka's West Arm Bay. The Titan Deck adds strength, rigidity and stability along with a cool and slip-resistant surface for summer's bare feet.

FACING PAGE: Like all of our installations, the Western Red Cedar docks are constructed with a quality-first approach. Sitting on Lake Minnetonka's Crystal Bay, western cedar wood has been chosen by hand to give the dock its perfect appearance.
Photographs courtesy of Crepeau Docks

"Lake residents extend their homes by installing docks, raising the capacity for outdoor entertainment. They're an investment."

—Tim Niccum

ABOVE & FACING PAGE: We bought the company from the Crepeaus in 1987 and have expanded ever since. With a focus on service, our docks can come in any size. Whether it's a marina for 100 boats, a private residence dock or a small fishing dock, the installation can fit any occasion. Our dock will become part of your home. People often spend more time on their dock than on their boat. We also offer boat lifts, boathouses and accessories as a means of enjoying Minnesota's scenic lakes and rivers.

Photographs courtesy of Crepeau Docks

"Simplicity is sometimes the most elegant; quiet details often have the most appeal."

—Bob Swanson

ABOVE LEFT: The design elements should reflect the homeowners' taste and style; the details will enhance and complement the homes' architecture. The custom colored, multiple sized, textured and tumbled pavers used were chosen to match the natural stone on the home, highlighted with a coordinating light colored non-textured border.
Photograph by Lecy Design

ABOVE RIGHT: Patterns in the pavement direct lines of sight. A traditional Minnesota home with contemporary flair by Steve Kleineman uses a herringbone pattern to direct the eye toward the front entry. The one size, larger scale non-tumbled paver achieves a crisp, clean look. Custom blended driveway pavers pull out the green-brown hues of the slate roof with a change of scale and texture on the border and front entry plaza.
Photograph by Lecy Design

FACING PAGE: As the paving industry has grown in the last decade, Americans have come to expect more choices—something we embrace. Colors, textures and shapes can be made to fit nearly any architectural taste, and should last a lifetime. On this Charles Stinson-designed home, we used a pewter and charcoal palette, letting the dynamics of the home take center stage. With such an upscale and elegant roofline, the pavement surrounding the house should simply complement it.
Photograph by Jim Gallop

"Knowing the history of this 5,000-year-old craft makes the results even more rewarding. Since Roman times, we've used stone and clay to pave the world's infrastructure—a necessity that's crucial to a society's success."

—Bob Swanson

ABOVE LEFT: Kevin Streeter—Streeter & Associates—partnered with architect David Salmela to create this award-winning project. The architectural design favors light and simplicity. Located in Deephaven, the home's exterior space follows the modern style of David's work by using a non-tumbled large scaled paver—laid in a half bond running pattern—emulating the simplicity, scale and pattern of the home's exterior. Minimalism shines, as the design highlights the sophistication of the architecture and lets natural light play a prominent role. The straightforward, clean landscaping furthers the effect—an element that is always factored into our plans. Outdoor greenery has the ability to impact the feeling of a home.
Photograph by Lecy Design

ABOVE RIGHT: A classic Bruce Schmidt design features a multiple-level outdoor dining space utilizing a multiple sized, soft tumbled stone-like paver. Stone columns and balusters accent the style of the outdoor gathering spot creating a quiet, lighter, elegant setting.
Photograph by Lecy design

FACING PAGE: Nothing could have captured the Old World charm of a Victorian home like the simplicity of the herringbone pattern. Appropriately constructed with a "Purington" reclaimed street paver, the driveway allows the home to appear just as it would have 150 years ago.
Photograph by Jim Gallop

"Why should Minnesotans enjoy the outdoors any less than Californians? Our kitchens extend the possibilities for everyone."

—Michael Anderson

ABOVE: Each installation fits the personality of the family, whether it's a comprehensive kitchen or a fire pit. Fueled with propane or natural gas, the fire pits can be placed on wooden decks, back patios or directly on the ground and feature galvanized and stainless steel components. Whether stucco or tile, they add an unexpected element to a simple evening at home—bonfires, cookouts or pure atmosphere, the options are unlimited.

FACING PAGE: Dinner parties take on a whole new life; a full outdoor installation lets the host store, prepare and cook without leaving the guests.
Photographs courtesy of Minnesota Seasons

"We can create any outdoor kitchen with endless options."
—Michael Anderson

ABOVE: I spend much of my free time outside, which has been a helpful factor in developing ways for people to enjoy their backyards. Bar-height fire pits with dining space allow family and visitors to eat and drink comfortably—even on a chilly Minnesota night.
Photograph courtesy of Minnesota Seasons

FACING PAGE TOP: A complete kitchen includes every indoor component the cook may want, including a grill, refrigerator, bartender and many other options—even an outdoor television. Think your outdoor dream kitchen is too big to install? Impossible. If it is not accessible manually, we can crane our products into the backyard, freeing ourselves from restrictions that may appear during other methods of construction.
Photograph courtesy of Vintage Luxury Outdoor Appliances

FACING PAGE BOTTOM: For a family who does a good deal of entertaining and has children, we placed a kitchen next to the swimming pool and in sight of the children's play area, calling it the "stay-cation." The 11-foot umbrella and bar lets friends comfortably chat with the cook, all within close range of the kids. Fitting beautifully with their home, the kitchen features custom colors to match the patio.
Photograph courtesy of Minnesota Seasons

OLYMPIC POOLS

Shakopee, Minnesota

"No matter how much you enjoy your pool, you will have many more hours of pleasure viewing, relaxing or entertaining around the pool. That's why we work closely with the owners and landscape designers to ensure the pool or spa complements their family, lifestyle and landscaping plan."

—Jerry Kalin

ABOVE: We renovated an existing pool to add a spa that overflows into the pool, a bench, new equipment and raised the floor of the pool from nine to five feet. Working closely with a landscape contractor to ensure the cohesiveness of the project, we created a space perfect for this family's backyard oasis. The homeowners can enjoy their pool from April to October, whether swimming, lounging or cooking out. As a comfort to parents, an underwater ultrasound alarm system was installed to generate an audible alarm if a child falls into the pool.

FACING PAGE: A freeform shape with black plaster was used to create the look of a natural pond at the bottom of a quarry. The pool features generous lengths of steps and benches in the pool for relaxing, a tanning rock, underwater lighting directed vertically at the overhanging rocks, extra skimmers to keep the pool clean and a waterfall rock with adjustable water flow. Out of more than 900 pools, this pool won a prestigious *Gold Medal* in the annual Association of Pool and Spa Professionals, APSP, *Awards of Excellence* competition. *Photographs courtesy of Olympic Pools*

"We've been doing this since 1983; we know how to build unique pools that make sense for families. Lifestyle should always be reflected in the design."

—Jerry Kalin

ABOVE: The back of an H-shaped home found a perfect match with a five-foot-deep pool and adjacent spa. Overlooking the lake, the pool and spa area is perfect for the owners and their grandchildren because of its shallow waters and the surrounding lush green grass.

FACING PAGE TOP: A backyard with limited space requires a design that maximizes the use of the area. An outdoor kitchen and attachable basketball hoop make this area ideal for family gatherings. LED lighting provides evening colors, while lighted laminar jets and thoughtful landscaping give the pool a special look in the evenings, perfect for summer pool parties or entertaining.

FACING PAGE BOTTOM: Built in a concrete coffer due to its proximity to water and a high water table, this five-foot-deep pool is adjacent to a popular lake. Extra steps at the end of the pool and a bench that runs its entire length make it an ideal pool to relax, visit and view the summer activities on the lake.
Photographs courtesy of Olympic Pools

"We do for the earth what doctors do for the sick. Our patient is the land; restoring and maintaining the health of local plant communities is our top priority."

—Ron Bowen

ABOVE: A home landscape captures the allure of the Minnesota prairie in July, set in the Minneapolis suburb of Plymouth. We created a garden—a concept that includes selected elements and careful design to accurately represent the natural prairie.
Photograph by Mike Evenocheck

FACING PAGE: With the nation's growing awareness of ecological concerns, companies have been moving toward presenting a strong image of compassion. When we worked with the leadership of the Lake Region Electric Cooperative in central Minnesota, they wanted to show their care and concern for indigenous preservation.
Photograph by Ron Bowen

"Sincerity lies at the heart of the company. We started with genuine compassion, a logical idea and the sturdiness of my old pick-up truck. And the sentiment has caught on—society notices the importance of what we've been doing for more than 30 years."

—Ron Bowen

ABOVE LEFT: The prairie is a delicate ecosystem, storing soil and carbon to nurture flora and fauna. A midsummer scene demonstrates this as a Monarch butterfly sits amongst butterfly milkweed, pink phlox and black-eyed Susans.

ABOVE RIGHT: We gave charm to an open, rural residential site with careful orientation of each plant. Butterfly milkweed, vervain and yellow coreopsis grow to the edge of the landowner's home.

FACING PAGE: My background has given me the tools to focus on the biological aspect of our work. Studies in forestry and a master's degree in landscape architecture have given me a technical base to work from and allow me to share the appeal of the land, in both function and form. A tallgrass prairie was restored for both conservation and aesthetic purposes. The open countryside shows off prairie phlox and a variety of grasses in June.
Photographs by Ron Bowen

perspectives
ON DESIGN

MINNESOTA TEAM
ASSOCIATE PUBLISHER: Heidi Nessa
GRAPHIC DESIGNER: Ashley DuPree
EDITOR: Katrina Autem
PRODUCTION COORDINATOR: Drea Williams

HEADQUARTERS TEAM
PUBLISHER: Brian G. Carabet
PUBLISHER: John A. Shand
EXECUTIVE PUBLISHER: Phil Reavis
DIRECTOR OF DEVELOPMENT & DESIGN: Beth Benton Buckley
DIRECTOR OF BOOK MARKETING & DISTRIBUTION: Julia Hoover
PUBLICATION MANAGER: Lauren B. Castelli
SENIOR GRAPHIC DESIGNER: Emily A. Kattan
GRAPHIC DESIGNER: Kendall Muellner
EDITORIAL DEVELOPMENT SPECIALIST: Elizabeth Gionta
MANAGING EDITOR: Rosalie Z. Wilson
EDITOR: Anita M. Kasmar
EDITOR: Daniel Reid
MANAGING PRODUCTION COORDINATOR: Kristy Randall
PRODUCTION COORDINATOR: Laura Greenwood
TRAFFIC COORDINATOR: Meghan Anderson
ADMINISTRATIVE MANAGER: Carol Kendall
ADMINISTRATIVE ASSISTANT: Beverly Smith
CLIENT SUPPORT COORDINATOR: Amanda Mathers

PANACHE PARTNERS, LLC
CORPORATE HEADQUARTERS
1424 Gables Court
Plano, TX 75075
469.246.6060
www.panache.com

John Kraemer and Sons Inc., page 97

index

THE PANACHE COLLECTION

CREATING SPECTACULAR PUBLICATIONS FOR DISCERNING READERS

Dream Homes Series
An Exclusive Showcase of the Finest Architects, Designers and Builders

Carolinas
Chicago
Coastal California
Colorado
Deserts
Florida
Georgia
Los Angeles
Metro New York
Michigan
Minnesota

New England
New Jersey
Northern California
Ohio & Pennsylvania
Pacific Northwest
Philadelphia
South Florida
Southwest
Tennessee
Texas
Washington, D.C.

Spectacular Homes Series
An Exclusive Showcase of the Finest Interior Designers

California
Carolinas
Chicago
Colorado
Florida
Georgia
Heartland
London
Michigan
Minnesota
New England

New York
Ohio & Pennsylvania
Pacific Northwest
Philadelphia
South Florida
Southwest
Tennessee
Texas
Toronto
Washington, D.C.
Western Canada

Perspectives on Design Series
Design Philosophies Expressed by Leading Professionals

Carolinas
Chicago
Colorado
Florida
Georgia
London

Minnesota
New England
Pacific Northwest
San Francisco
Southwest

City by Design Series
An Architectural Perspective

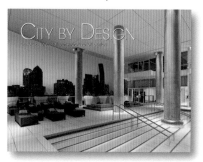

Atlanta
Charlotte
Chicago
Dallas
Denver
Orlando
Phoenix
San Francisco
Texas

Spectacular Wineries Series
A Captivating Tour of Established, Estate and Boutique Wineries

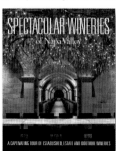

California's Central Coast
Napa Valley
New York
Sonoma Country

Art of Celebration Series
The Making of a Gala

Florida Style
New York Style
Washington, D.C. Style

Specialty Titles

Distinguished Inns of North America
Extraordinary Homes California

Spectacular Golf of Colorado
Spectacular Golf of Texas
Spectacular Hotels

Spectacular Restaurants of Texas
Visions of Design

Panache Partners, LLC   1424 Gables Court   Plano, Texas 75075   469.246.6060   www.panache.com